The
DISCIPLESHIP
SERIES

The DISCIPLESHIP SERIES
THE BEGINNINGS

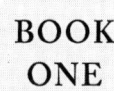

BOOK ONE

MIKE ADKINS

The Discipleship Series: Book One
Copyright © 2015 by Mike Adkins. All rights reserved.

No part of this publication may be reproduced, stored in a retrieval system or transmitted in any way by any means, electronic, mechanical, photocopy, recording or otherwise without the prior permission of the author except as provided by USA copyright law.

This book is designed to provide accurate and authoritative information with regard to the subject matter covered. This information is given with the understanding that neither the author nor Tate Publishing, LLC is engaged in rendering legal, professional advice. Since the details of your situation are fact dependent, you should additionally seek the services of a competent professional.

The opinions expressed by the author are not necessarily those of Tate Publishing, LLC.

Published by Tate Publishing & Enterprises, LLC
127 E. Trade Center Terrace | Mustang, Oklahoma 73064 USA
1.888.361.9473 | www.tatepublishing.com

Tate Publishing is committed to excellence in the publishing industry. The company reflects the philosophy established by the founders, based on Psalm 68:11,
"The Lord gave the word and great was the company of those who published it."

Book design copyright © 2015 by Tate Publishing, LLC. All rights reserved.
Cover design by Nikolai Purpura and Zachery Adkins
Interior design by Mary Jean Archival

Published in the United States of America

ISBN: 978-1-68028-326-6
1. Religion / Christian Life / Personal Growth
2. Religion / Christian Ministry / Discipleship
15.08.07

Acknowledgments

Sometimes, as I have read this page in books I'm reading, I've wondered why the author needed to thank so many people. I now realize this type of thing is a collective effort! Please allow me the space to say thanks to many supporters.

From the first days when God began to deal with me about this book series, I struggled to accept my responsibility and role. As I rewrite this page years into the project, I still struggle with, "Are you sure You want *me* to do this, Lord?" In those earliest days, my mom Patricia Adkins, and my close friend Rev. Herschal Holly, in heaven now, were true encouragements! I might never have seriously started if not for their constant urging, prayer, and follow-up.

Many other people deserve credit. My wife, Martha, has played a critical role of support, even in the midst of her own PhD process! My children—Tracy, Mandy, Jennifer, Zachery, Micah—and now some sons-in-laws and grandchildren have prayed and put up with me being "otherwise occupied" for a long time, even sometimes on vacation. Rev. Keith Grove and Lloyd Stines did reviews for me. I hesitate to mention family and friends who have prayed and helped in many ways, but I must mention some: Bob and Vic,

Tim and Mert, Sandy, friends Diane and Mike, Bill, Mike, Paul, Ed and Shelly, Dr. Jonah Mitchell, Dr. Stan Toler, brother and sister-in-law Rev. Mark and Margret Reynolds, and Dr. David Case. I know many friends and parishioners have prayed and I say, "Thank you!"

I have been and am humbled more than I can say that God would ever ask me to do such a thing! I am not worthy. I've struggled to grow in areas of my own life. I'm sure some will find faults and mistakes with the book and with me. I've given it my best. I praise Him for His supreme wisdom and help! *I have only undertaken this for Him and the growth of His children!*

Contents

Preface 11
   The Decision 11
   Expectations 13
   Purpose of the Book 14

1 Your Commitment 19
   Spiritual History 21
   Justification-Forgiveness 26
   Sincerity with God 28
   Family of God 30
   Importance of the Step You Have Taken 31
   Public Witness of Becoming a Christian 33
   Baptism 35
   Begin to Live Christlike 37
   Depend Upon God 39

2 Prayer 41
   Prayer: Who and What 43
   Conversation 44

 Prayer: When 45
 Prayer: Where 48
 Prayer: How 50
 Sincerity 51
 Faith/Belief/Trust 52
 Scriptural Power: Prayer Promises 53
 Prayer: Why 56

3 Faith 61
 Definitions 63
 History 68
 Developing Our Faith 73

4 Sharing Your God 77
 Introduction 79
 God's Command 80
 What Others Do (Or Not Do) 82
 How to Share 84
 Motivation to Share 87

5 Bible Study/Devotions 91
 Devotions 95
 Bible Study 98

6 Christian Associations 103
 Introduction 105
 You Are Your Environment 105
 Nature 108
 Reward/Defeat 111
 Association Controls 112

7 Be Conscious of God's Leadership 115
 Introduction 117

- *God's Plan for Your Life* 118
- *The Dependency Paradox* 123
- *How This Works Against Us* 123
- *Finding God's Will* 125
- *Formula for Knowing God's Will* 126
- *God Will Not Forsake You* 131
- *Listen and Obey* 132

8 Your Pastor/Discipler 133
- *Roles of the Pastor/Discipler* 135
- *Christ, the Discipler* 142
- *Your Roles* 143
- *Watch Christ* 147

9 Giving to God 151
- *Author's Challenge* 153
- *Again, God's Plan for the World:*
  Your Part 154
- *Time* 159
- *Money* 161
- *You Can't Out-Give God* 163
- *Where Do You Put*
  Your Time, Talent, and Tithe? 166
- *Self* 168

10 Wolves in Sheep's Clothing 171
- *Introduction* 173
- *Good vs. Evil* 175
- *Sidetracked* 178
- *Christlikeness* 182

Conclusion 185

Study Guides 189

Preface

The Decision

Greetings, fellow Christian! You have joined the pilgrimage, the trek to heaven! How exciting! There's a lot to learn! We might as well get started now.

Welcome to the real world! Perhaps you have already begun to experience some effects of this new walk, perhaps not. The purpose of this study is to help you make that transition from life without Christ to the Christian walk. I'll tell you here, and now, it's not always easy! In fact, many times, it's really hard! In Ephesians 6:10–13 (NIV), the Apostle Paul says, "Finally be strong in the Lord and in His mighty power. Put on the full armor of God so that you can take your stand against the devil's schemes. For our struggle is not against flesh and blood, but against the rulers, against the authorities, against the powers of this dark world and against the spiritual forces of evil in the heavenly realms. Therefore put on the full armor of God, so that when the day of evil comes, you may be able to stand your ground, and after you have done everything, to stand." This is the real world and the task before you! I want to help you through this study, to "put on the full armor of God."

By asking Jesus Christ to forgive your sins and accepting Him into your heart, you have stepped into this real world. Hopefully you have bid good-bye to your past and are looking forward to this new walk with Christ! As you accepted Him, you did become a new creation (2 Corinthians 5.17). The blood of Jesus Christ shed on the cross has cleansed your heart from all sins committed, and He has given you a new beginning! He has helped you to choose to cross that line separating good and evil. You are a believer! That is exciting!

I'll also tell you right here at the start, many people would have you follow "their" brand of Christianity, and so the difficulty comes from not only the devil but sometimes from within the church itself. Their intentions are usually good, but one must be careful. Some would have you believe salvation is about your clothes, your hairstyle, your style of baptism, your friends, your habits, or your talk. And in one way or another, all of these things may eventually factor into your spiritual life. But this step you have taken to accept Jesus Christ is about faith and forgiveness! *Jesus understands you and accepts you just as you are!* John 3:17 says, "For God did not send His Son into the world to condemn the world, but that the world through him might be saved." Jesus is not out to condemn you (John 8:1–11)! If you sincerely asked God to forgive your sins, He did! You are saved! You are a new Christian! You have made the definitive step away from the devil and this world toward Christ and everlasting life! Don't let the devil or anyone else talk you out of that position. Trust God! He is fair and just!

This decision you have made to accept Christ into your heart is the most important decision you have or ever will make. The Creator God of the universe has reached down. You have taken His hand and stepped into a new life! Keep on trusting the One who has brought you this far—Jesus!

Expectations

When you became a new Christian, something changed about you that many new Christians do not handle well. Everyone now will expect something of you. That's right. They are watching and now expecting. Your churchgoing friends will expect you never to miss church and comment if you do. Your boss may expect you to work over every time you are asked because it's the Christian thing to do. Your coworkers may expect you to never make a mistake and razz you when you do. Your family may expect you never to show anger and wag their heads when you do. Beginning to get the picture? You just think you do! Your Sunday School teacher may expect you to read all those Old Testament names out loud in class. Your pastor may expect you to take on some task for the church. Some Bible Study leader may want you to "share" in a session. The little widowed saint down the street may want you to take her to the store, even if it is your only free night of the week. And that family in the church with the children my kids would call the "demon children" (actually happened) will want you to babysit every time there is a gospel concert in town. They may even call you a selfish hypocrite if you ever refuse. Now you get the picture, right? Wrong!

Won't you have some expectations for yourself? You will naturally feel guilty when you miss church; say no to your boss, the pastor, and the widowed saint; make a mistake at work; show anger toward a family member; flub-up those names in Sunday. school class; not share in Bible Study; or refuse to babysit the demon kids! Of course, you will feel bad! That's the devil's business. You will, of course, want to seriously pray, read your Bible every day, consistently attend church, and witness to others but will fail at all these sometimes! Maybe even seriously fail sometimes! You will not meet all the expectations you have for yourself. But finally, you are getting the picture, right? Wrong again!

God has some expectations for you! Whoa! What? That's right! Stop and rethink this scenario! The only expectations here you must satisfy to remain a Christian are God's! Ironically, He probably expects less from you than all of the others. Not that He doesn't want progress from you; He does! But He is patient, kind, uncondemning, helpful, and understanding! Focus on God and His expectations!

About the others? Some of them will be important, but prioritize and review. Learn soon to say no! Make sure God is pleased with your life! He is who is important! Be polite and courteous, cautious not to offend but sensible at the same time! *Keep your eyes and ears upon Christ, and let the actions and comments of others go by the wayside!* Make your personal expectations high but accomplishable. God is fair and just. Watch and listen to Him!

Just a technical note: I urge you, as you read, to look up and read the parenthetical (example: James 2:7) scripture references. This will slow down your reading process but will greatly enhance your understanding of God and His Word. Again, that is the goal!

Purpose of the Book

It is the purpose of this book to help the new Christian convert gain practical and spiritual insight for understanding of the Word and ways of God, and thereby to grow. Without this type of help, this insight might only be gained slowly, or if the devil had his way, never at all. Hopefully, this book can act as a catalyst to keep the growth process moving ahead. If the progress of a Christian slows and stops, the Christian begins to die. The Christian walk is much like a person going upstream in a canoe. The canoe will continue to make progress only as long as the occupant continues to paddle. If the person grows tired and rests, the canoe's progress immediately slows and stops and then begins to flow downstream with the current of water. Similarly, the Christian must always, with God's help, of course, be making progress—growing—or he/she begins to slow, stop, and flow backward with the flow of the world.

In Matthew 7:13–14 (NKJV) is a picture that helps us here. Jesus is speaking and says, "Enter by the narrow gate; for wide is the gate and broad is the way that leads to destruction, and there are many who go in by it. Because narrow is the gate and difficult is the way which leads to life, and there are few who find it." I picture the narrow way as a path that flows up the middle of the broad and wide way. It flows opposite of the broad and wide way. The narrow way goes against the current. It is a difficult way. One must always be stroking the spiritual paddle. If one quits paddling, the current pulls us immediately in the other direction.

It is the devil's business to cause the Christians, and especially the New Christians, to slow and tire of paddling. Whenever you see a Christian fall or backslide, mark it down that it did not "just" happen. It was a process of slowing down spiritually until they allowed the devil to stop them completely. Then they began to flow in the opposite direction. Continued spiritual growth and forward movement is difficult at times but critical to spiritual life! I hope this book will bring insight for understanding and, therefore, growth because the underlying intention is to disciple.

Someone, somewhere, some time, planted the seed of spirituality in your life. Someone watered that seed, and it has now sprung into the life of salvation. I hope now this book can help with the process of maturation and growth. I hope, through the knowledge contained herein, and with the help and guidance of the Holy Spirit of God, to help you survive spiritually that critical infancy period. Spiritual failure is common, the odds are difficult, and the devil is fighting against you! In Jesus's example of the Parable of the Sower or Soils in Matthew 13, four spiritual seeds are planted, yet only one survives the critical infant period to become a productive adult Christian. The seed falling by the wayside or hard ground is like the gospel being heard by a person without spiritual understanding. Because they have no background, the understanding comes slow. The devil comes quickly and steals the opportunity away with temptations, fears, and false explanations before it has opportunity to take root and grow. The seed falling on rocky ground is like the gospel being heard by a person with only a little spiritual background and little depth of spiritual knowledge. The gospel seed does spring to life. However, because of fear, confusion, or no help from someone to guide them, the new Christian does not get their spiritual roots established before the devil comes. Like the hot sun on a plant with little root system, the devil tricks them and brings offence to them, and they wither spiritually and lose out with God. The seed falling into thorny ground is like the gospel being heard by a person wrapped up in the everyday cares and riches of this life. Spiritual life springs forth in their life but only to be choked back by the direction of their focus. The devil sidetracks them with car payments, doctor bills, and work promotions of this world, and they never become fruitful for God. Finally, the one in four seeds is like the gospel being received by one who has some background and wants to thrive for God. This person maximizes their opportunity and focuses on growing in the Lord. They do grow and become fruitful for God. This seems to be the desired standard. What can make the difference? When Jesus planted twelve seeds of the gospel within His followers, the disciples, only one was lost. What is this difference? Discipling!

Hopefully this book, again with God's help, will assist you and others to have a beginning understanding of spiritual things. Hopefully, it will help you get down early spiritual roots, pull away from the singular focus of this life, and grow toward Christ enough to survive this initial infant period. You can overcome with God! "with God all things are possible!" (Matthew 19.26, KJV).

Now remember, even with the seed that became fruitful, difficult times had to be faced. So when those times come for you, whether discouragement, temptations, lack of understanding, or whatever, go to your pastor! He/she will be understanding and will help you on this road to getting established spiritually.

I hope you are excited! It is a challenging time spiritually, but you have embarked on the…bar none, mind you…on the most rewarding journey of your life! Make your mind up, whatever you must face, with God's help. You not only can but will survive to live with Jesus here and hereafter! The will to survive spiritually is just as important here as your physical will to live.

You are going to make it! I believe in you! I am praying for you! God bless!

Again, an author's technical note: please, I urge you as you read to look up and read the parenthetical scripture references (example: James 2:7). This will slow down your reading process but will greatly enhance your understanding of God and His Word!

And again, that is the goal!

1

Your Commitment

"Commit your way to the Lord; trust in Him and He will do this: He will make your righteousness shine like the dawn, the justice of your cause like the noonday sun."
—Psalm 37:5–6 (NIV)

Your Commitment

Spiritual History

In this first chapter, let's take a few moments to look at your spiritual history and heritage. From where did all this spiritual opportunity derive? What does the Bible tell us of the events leading up to your conversion? Let us take a quick overview.

We know that, in the beginning, God created heaven and earth and mankind. But prior to that, God had, for an unspecified period of time, lived with created beings—angels. Although all this is not explained in detail, there is enough scripture for us to understand. God, in some way, became dissatisfied with the arrangement He had with the angels. In some way, the sovereign God decided to give His angels a choice, as He did later with mankind. We don't know exactly how it happened, but we do know Lucifer decided to do wrong. Many of the angels, about one-third, decided to follow Lucifer and tried to overthrow God, the Word, in heaven. This, of course, failed; Lucifer became God's archenemy, and He and His followers were ejected from heaven (Isaiah 14:12–16; Ezekiel 28:12–19; 2 Peter 2:4). God continued with His plan for earth and mankind and also gave mankind a choice about following after and loving God. The devil, as Lucifer came to be known, claimed the earth as his domain and struggles to this day to interfere with mankind's relationship with God. His hate for God drives him to try to lead mankind astray and get him not to follow after and love God. You're familiar with the story of the Garden of Eden, where God allowed the devil to tempt Adam and Eve, His first human creations.

God had created Adam and Eve in His own image and likeness with a deep desire to worship a Higher Being. But God had also balanced that desire with the ability to reason and with something called "free moral agency," the right to choose for themselves. Thus, mankind had the mental capacity to think a process through and the right to make His own decision about whether or not he would serve God. Although not specifically stated as such in the Bible, it is clear from the incident with Lucifer and the angels, and now with Adam and Eve, God wants us to choose to love and follow Him.

The stage was set. Adam and Eve walked and talked with God every day in the Garden but were also given an "off-limits" tree from which they were not to eat. Along came the devil and presented Eve with the temptation to eat from that forbidden tree. God now had His desired test; mankind would make a choice. Eve, and then Adam, chose to eat of the fruit and to disobey God. God had given to Adam and Eve only a few instructions, one limitation, and a promised judgment if they violated the limitation. They had exercised their right of free moral choice. Mankind had failed God's first test.

Then God, true to His word as always, proceeded to follow through with a plan of judgment. There were many consequences to man's choice, such as being driven out of the Garden, having to grow their own food, weeds, thorns, human disease, increased childbirth pain, and so on (Genesis 3), but the most significant, where we are concerned for this study, was the ongoing curse of inborn sin that continues to affect every person born into the world, even to this very day (Romans 5:12–21). This inborn sin, put very simply, is a part of our spiritual nature at birth. It is the nature within us that makes us want our own way. This nature is the single explanation as to why mankind instinctively continues to move away from God. All of mankind is so affected, as is the universe we live in, so everything we know naturally deteriorates rather than regenerates. It moves away from God. This is our condition as non-Christians in this world. We have no natural inclination moving us toward God.

God took all this into mind when He created this world. He knew in advance, through His all-knowing nature, what mankind's choice would be, and He made provision for mankind's forgiveness and salvation.

Slowly, God began to show Himself to mankind to try and help mankind understand God. Throughout the Old Testament, we see God reaching down to mankind. For instance, early on, we see Noah building a huge boat that said in effect to his neighbors, "God is still in charge, even if you have forgotten Him." In his comparatively small society, everyone knew what Noah was doing and why he was doing it. They didn't believe him, but God was still trying to reach down to mankind. God became so frustrated with mankind at this time He destroyed life in the world with a great flood. Only Noah, his family, and the animals within the ark survived, and then God started over (Genesis 6–9).

Now God tried a different methodology: He chose a certain man for Himself and decided to "grow" Himself a people. He had not been successful at reaching mankind as a whole, so now the plan had some limitations. If He could reach one person, perhaps through that person, He could reach other persons. Then through those persons, perhaps He could reach peoples; and then through those peoples, perhaps He could reach a nation; and then through a nation, perhaps He could reach the world. And so God began again the slow process of trying to bring mankind back to Himself.

Again, look at God as He reached down to mankind throughout the history of the Old Testament. God chose to work with Abram, who came to be called Abraham, because of his belief in God to "grow" Himself a people. God promised and then miraculously provided a son to Abraham and Sarah through which these people would come. We see an angel appearing to Jacob; God using Joseph to protect these *people*; the "family" flourishing in Egypt; Moses responding to the burning bush; Israel, now a massive "nation" being lead out of Egypt; pillars of fire; God on the mountain; laws to follow; the promised land; Joshua; Jericho; God fighting battles for Israel; David, the king; and God in the temple; etc., for all the world to watch (early Old Testament). God's love constantly motivated Him to reach out to mankind, to relentlessly try to help mankind, to understand God.

Then with "For God so loved the world that He gave His only begotten Son" (John 3:16, KJV), Jesus appeared upon earth as God's ultimate attempt to reach out to mankind. God Himself, in the person of His Son, was born into the world as a human in an effort for God to know mankind and for mankind to understand God. In this effort, as planned by God in His original plan of action, Jesus was put to death on the cross. The very *people* that God had been *growing* and reaching out to all those thousands of years rejected Jesus as the Messiah and put Him to death. This, however, provided for each of us the necessary sacrifice to allow mankind to have forgiveness of sin because God now again widened His outreach efforts to include all people.

My older brother passed along this story one Sunday morning that Paul Harvey had told on his national broadcast, and it helps me illustrate where God was here.

> The Christmas Story…the God-born-in-a-manger and all that…escapes some moderns. Mostly, I think, because they seek complex answers to their questions, and this one is so utterly simple. For the cynics, the skeptics and the unconvinced, I submit a modern parable.

This is about a modern man. One of us.

He was not a Scrooge. He was a kind, decent, mostly good man. Generous to his family, upright in his dealings with other men. But he did not believe in all that Incarnation stuff which churches proclaim at Christmas time. It just did not make sense and he was too honest to pretend otherwise.

He just could not swallow the Jesus story. About God coming to earth as a man.

"I'm truly sorry to distress you," he told his wife, "but I'm not going to church with you this Christmas Eve." He said he'd feel like a hypocrite. That he would much rather stay home. But that he would wait up for them.

He stayed. They went.

Shortly after the family drove away in the car, snow began to fall.

He went to the window to watch the flurries getting heavier and heavier, then went back to his fireside chair and began to read his newspaper.

Minutes later he was startled by a thudding sound. Then another, then another.

At first, he thought someone must be throwing snowballs against his living room window.

When he went to the front door to investigate, he found a flock of birds huddled miserably in the snow. They had been caught in the storm and in a desperate search for shelter had tried to fly through his large landscape window. Well…he couldn't let the poor creatures lie there and die.

He remembered the barn where his children stabled their pony. That would provide warm shelter if he could direct the birds to it.

He quickly put on his coat, galoshes. Tramped through the deepening snow to the barn.

He opened the doors wide and turned on the light.

But the birds did not come in.

He figured food would entice them in and he hurried back to the house, fetched breadcrumbs, sprinkled them on the snow, making a trail to the yellow-lighted wide-open doorway of the stable.

But to his dismay the birds ignored the breadcrumbs and continued to flop around helplessly in the snow.

He tried catching them.

He tried shooing them into the barn by walking around waving his arms. Instead they scattered in every direction—except into the warm lighted barn.

Then he realized they were afraid of him. "To them," he reasoned, "I am a strange and terrifying creature. If only I could think of some way to let them know they can trust me, that I am not trying to hurt them, but to help them."

How?

Any move he made tended to frighten them, confuse them. They just would not follow....they would not be led or shooed because they feared him.

If only I could be a bird myself, he thought.

If only I could be a bird and mingle with them and speak their language and tell them not to be afraid and show them the way to the safe, warm barn.

But I'd have to be one of them...so they could see...and hear and understand...

At that moment, the church bells began to ring. The sounds reached his ears above the sounds of the wind.

He stood there...listening to the bells...Adeste Fidelis...listening to the bells pealing the glad tidings of Christmas.

And he sank to his knees in the snow.

Justification-Forgiveness

In God's original plan, He set up judgments and requirements if sin was committed. Sin had to be punished. God's requirements of justice could not and cannot simply be ignored. Sin was set up as punishable by death. So to satisfy God the Father's sense of justice, a death must occur. So for God to keep His word and to satisfy His justice system, all of mankind, born with sin in their hearts because of Adam and Eve's sin and the subsequent curse, must die. Or God had to provide an alternate death that would suffice for all of mankind's sins or that would justify mankind. Down through time, many sacrifices were allowed by God, but none of them would actually atone for the sins of mankind. Jesus, the very Son of God, in an effort to reach out to mankind once again, would provide the ultimate sacrifice. Only He could provide a sacrifice that would be sufficient enough to allow for justification within God's justice system. Justification, simply put, means to qualify the guilty one "just as if he/she had never sinned." Jesus died on the cross for you and me and for all people of the world (John 3:16–17). With that death of the Son of God, the death mandate of God the Father's was satisfied, and mankind's right to choose was preserved. Now, as in the past, we can choose to go our way and not serve God and His rules, or with the atonement made for our sins by Christ on the cross, we can find forgiveness (justification) and follow God by our own choice. Even though Adam and Eve broke relations with God, God's plan of action is still in effect, and He is still reaching out to mankind, just as you have experienced.

You will not find human perfectness in this forgiveness process. You will continue to make mistakes and to be vulnerable to sin. (Therefore the bumper sticker saying: "Not Perfect, Just Forgiven.") Adam and Eve were perfect humans, given only one limitation, and still broke God's heart. Our tendency, remember, is toward deterioration. God has for you a great deal of help, but you will still have to work at the process of resisting temptation. For instance, you will hurt someone's feelings by something you should not have said. Perhaps your attitude will be wrong. Maybe you are working at breaking wrongful habits like taking God's name in vain and will slip and curse again. You will probably have to tell someone you are sorry and say to God, "I'm sorry. Please forgive me," but He will readily forgive you if you are sincere.

So you are forgiven. Someone else (Jesus) took your place in death and punishment, and that is what is behind you by way of history. Your heart, which was stained with the record of the sins you had committed, is now completely clean. There is no record against you since you have been forgiven (justified) and your name is written in the Lamb's Book of Life (Revelation 21:27). You have not been forgiven for sins you have not yet committed; that would be illogical—"cart before the horse" kind of thing—but neither do you *have* to sin! You will since you are not humanly perfect, but Jesus is patient and will forgive you (Hebrews 4:14–16) when you fail, if you are sincere and continue to try. You will never be physically or humanly perfect, but you can be spiritually perfect and acceptable in God's eyes as long as you back up, correct mistakes, and continue to be sincere with God.

Sincerity with God

That is how God sees us, you know. He looks on our heart (1 Samuel 16:7). The reading to follow here is pretty heady discourse for New Christians but necessary to protect your soul from the tricks of the devil. Remember this is a learning process, and I'm trying to work in advance to help you with issues I believe you will face.

God can tell by looking at the attitude of our hearts just what or how we really feel. For instance, all of us have answered this question incorrectly more than once, "How are you today?" We say, "Fine, how are you?" Many times, of course, we are not fine. We may not feel physically well, may not be emotionally well, or may be sick about the fact we do not have the money to pay the house payment on time. But would we rarely, even ever, launch into a discourse about how we really are? Probably not! All of us have masked our feelings about a certain person or situation when it would not have been proper or beneficial to show our real feelings. You have done these? Okay, I'm not saying these things are sinful. I am saying that in any of these situations, God could look into our hearts and tell what we really felt or thought. And so, if we had been talking with God instead of with whomever, He would have known how we really felt when we said to Him with our mouth, "Fine, how are you?" He would have known how we really felt about Him when we shook his hand, smiled, and said, "Lovely party," instead of saying what we really felt like saying, "You have gross breath!" You get the picture? God looks on our hearts, and so He always knows the thoughts and intents of our heart and mind (Hebrews 4:12–13). We cannot fool God! You cannot say to God, "I am sorry for doing what I did. Please, forgive me," and find He forgives you, unless you really are sorrowful and sincere. He will know the motive of your request. It is one thing to be genuinely sorry for wrongdoing; it is quite another to be sorry for being caught. God knows the difference! Following here is a make-believe situation I hope will illustrate this point.

Let's say you and I met for coffee at a small restaurant. While we talked and sipped coffee, suddenly I slapped you in the face. Immediately, I say I am sorry and beg your forgiveness. I say you unexpectedly remind me of someone who had seriously offended me in the past, but I'm sorry and it will not happen again. Some of you reading this will not give me another chance but would leave the restaurant immediately and probably rightly so. Many of you reading this would forgive me, and we would continue to talk. Let's say, for the sake of the illustration, you all forgive me and we continue to talk and sip our coffee. A short time later, I slap you again! You are horrified, of course, and I break into tears and beg your forgiveness once again. I give the same excuse, say I am sorry and beg and beg for your forgiveness. Again, some of you would leave, saying I should seek professional help; some of you would slap me back. Others of you would forgive me, probably sympathize with me, and even try to console me. Again, let's say all of you forgive me and stay on to talk. It happens again, again, and again until all of you would sooner or later say, "You are not sorry, or you would quit slapping me!" And again, you would be correct! The same is true for God! God is patient and will forgive you, repeatedly if necessary, *but not if you are not sincere*! He looks on the heart and, sooner or later, will say, "You are not sorry, or you would stop hurting me!"

Not only do I urge you to not try and fool God, but I urge you to always be sincere with God. Just to say the words "I'm sorry" is not enough. Remember that God looks at your intent and really knows whether or not you are sorry. It is like two fighting children that you separate and then say to them, "Now say, 'I'm sorry.'" Many times, they do, but they put nothing into it and really don't mean it, so you say, "Do you really think Tommy believes that? Say it and act like you really are sorry." God always knows if you are sincere, and it does you no good if you are not.

That is some fairly heavyweight stuff to consider this early in the Christian walk, but I promise you will meet "Christians" who think they are fooling God. It's a trick of the devil no different than when He said to Eve, "Of course, you will not die. God know that as soon as you eat it your eyes will be opened and you will be like gods knowing both good and evil" Genesis 3:4–5 (NEB). Mixing some truth with the lie, the devil led Eve to fool herself and to think she could fool God. It can't be done!

Family of God

(Rom. 8:14–17)

When you accepted Jesus into your heart, you also accepted the Holy Spirit in some measure into your heart. (This is a more complex issue that we will deal with later in book 2.) For the moment, allow it to reflect that Jesus is not currently here in this world in the flesh but that we are led and directed by the Spirit of God (John 14:15–17). That, according to Paul in this Romans passage, allows us to be the sons and daughters of God, heirs to the kingdom of God, joint heirs with Jesus Christ. You are now a part of the family of God! Isn't that an exciting thought?

Paul, in some of his writings in the Bible, goes into some detailed explanations of how we are adopted through the blood of Jesus on the cross. The explanation is worthwhile, but for the moment, I want you to concentrate on the fact that you now belong to a family—the family of God. You have brothers and sisters all over the world. You have people who care about you who you don't even know. You will begin to care for others who you don't know. You will feel a kinship with those people as you grow in the Christian walk. To many Christians, this family becomes as close or closer to them as their physical family. You should be experiencing a great feeling of love from God and the family of God as you come to realize the magnitude of the fact you have become a family member. It is said that big families have lots of love. You have just joined perhaps the largest family in the world, and Jesus said in John 13:35 (ASV), "By this shall all men know that you are my disciples, if you have love one to another." Welcome to the family, brother or sister!

Importance of the Step You Have Taken

It is easy to get excited about becoming a Christian but not always easy to stay excited about being a Christian. I do not know, of course, how or where you became a Christian. Many times, it is in a church service, perhaps a revival meeting service, or perhaps some person led you to the Lord at home or on the job, but regardless of where, it was probably a time of stress and emotion as you made such a momentous decision. As God deals with our heart, which we generally refer to as being under conviction, we often (not everyone) feel our heart pound and experience a good deal of emotion because at the same time, the devil is making every effort to dissuade us from pledging ourselves to God. All this spiritual warfare creates within us that feeling of intensity and excitement. It is certainly not always the type of excitement that causes us to jump or shout but at least a type of stressful intensity as we make the decision to ask Jesus into out heart.

Now, from that position of the pounding heart, to today, you probably feel somewhat different. Maybe a great deal different. Perhaps even, the devil has made an effort to convince you that nothing really happened. Perhaps you have already worked through that. The point is you do not have to maintain the same level of heart-pounding excitement 100 percent of the time to remain a Christian. Jesus does not go away because the dynamics of your situation change from day to day.

All that to say this: Even though you feel different today than when you became a Christian, even though the devil may be trying to convince you that nothing really happened, even though the humdrum of everyday life may have caught back up with you, you did make a very important, life-changing decision! That decision was not a momentary one to be quickly discarded. It should be viewed as a decision you made to last a lifetime and beyond, into eternity! It should be viewed as a position that you wish to maintain for a lifetime or until Jesus returns.

The Bible puts this to us in a way that is not easy to forget. In the story of the Rich Fool (Lk 12:13–21), a man is made forgetful of his obligations to God because he has much of this world's goods. At the very time that he has forgotten he has an eternal soul, God requires his soul in judgment, and he is without God. Again, in Matthew 16:24–28 (KJV), Jesus is referring to the process of making a decision to follow Him, and He says "For what is a man profited, if he shall gain the whole world, and lose his own soul?" This decision you have made to follow Jesus is the most important decision you have or ever will make! Nothing—Nothing!—is more important than this decision and your personal relationship with Christ.

This decision that you made was one of the heart. You have embraced forgiveness from God and accepted Jesus into your heart. It can be a struggle to go from the atmosphere of the service or the stress and emotion of conviction to find mental acceptance of the decision that you have made. It is not always easy to hand over your sins of the past to an intangible God who you cannot actually see, hear, or touch and then believe in your head that Jesus is in your heart. It is a faith process. You must believe that God did do what He said He would do when you came to Him for forgiveness.

One thing that will help convince your head of what your heart has done is to tell someone what Jesus did for you. Let's look at the next section about public witness.

Public Witness of Becoming a Christian

You remember that within the original reasoning whereby God created mankind was for Him to receive voluntary love from a being. He was not satisfied with the love from the angels that He had created to love Him. That love was a love of obligation, not choice. God wanted something different! Now you have taken the step to accept Him as personal Lord and Savior voluntarily—just exactly what God longs for. He wants others to love Him out of choice. Would it seem appropriate then, knowing what God wants—others to love Him—for you to keep your relationship with Him a secret? Of course not!

Let's compare this to a relationship between a man and a woman. A couple falls in love and becomes engaged in a whirlwind romance. However, the man insists that no one know about their love for one another. He refuses to recognize her as his true love in public and acts ashamed or embarrassed if anyone questions him about her. Does he really love her? Should she marry him? The answer here is obvious, as is the comparison of your new love for Christ, I hope. Jesus wants you not to be ashamed of him. He wants you to be recognized as a Christian and for you to be a good example of what a Christian should be. Just as with the man and woman, everyone is watching.

Jesus speaks about this in the Bible, in Mark 8:38 (NEB), where He says "If anyone is ashamed of Me and mine in this wicked and godless age, the Son of Man (that's Jesus) will be ashamed of him, when He comes in the glory of His Father and of the holy angels." In other words, if we are ashamed of Jesus here and now and shun Him, He will be ashamed of us and shun us at the time of the rapture when He comes back for the church.

There are many ways of letting others know that you are a Christian. Your friends and close associates will probably know almost immediately because of the change in your person. This is a hard thing to describe if your personality already had some of the characteristics of most Christians but an easy thing to see if you have made many changes in the way that you talk or act or in your temperament. As you take on the actions and temperament of Christ, others around you will know that you are different without you saying anything.

For instance, I know of man in a church who I pastored who had a very bad temper. He would lose his temper very easily and did so on a regular basis. After he had become a Christian, grown in the Lord, and later accepted the Holy Spirit in sanctification (explained later in book 2), he was asking the Lord to open the door for him to witness to his work buddies, which he found difficult to do. It didn't take very long for God to answer. He was on a bowling team with men from his office and regularly lost his temper, but after this work of the Holy Spirit, he was different. The very next time that he bowled with them, they suddenly stopped in the middle of the game and questioned him as to why he was different and not loosing his temper. It was the perfect opportunity for him to witness, and he did. Again, as we begin to act more like Christ, others will know.

Years ago, when I was in the service, as we would train, I would bow my head and silently ask God to help me to do well. One day, a fellow recruit leaned close to me and said, "That's not fair. You are getting help." He was joking about the fact that I was praying, and I was honestly making no effort for others to see me. It was a witness to Him.

Sometimes, at work, at the family reunion, at a ball game, or wherever people congregate, a discussion will begin about God, church, or the end of time. These are opportunities not to force your beliefs on anyone but to tell them what God has done for you.

Sometimes, when someone is sick, has a flat tire, or needs help of any kind, that is the time to help and to accompany the help with a statement of your love for Christ, His love for them, and thus your motivation to help them.

When it is appropriate, don't be afraid to take a firm stand for Christ. You don't have to know all there is to know about the Bible or God, stick with what you do know. Give a strong testimony of what God *has done for you*. Life is shaped by the principles we live by. If we believe in nuclear disarmament, we don't hesitate to march, picket, or to do whatever to get our point heard. If we believe in saving the whales, then we send money, write letters, or go to Greenpeace and volunteer. Let's live the same way for Jesus! Learn about God and His ways, and don't be afraid to take a stand for what is right!

Baptism

Baptism is another way to let people know you have become a Christian. It is one of the sacraments of the church today. (A sacrament is simply a widely accepted spiritual practice that the church thinks should happen because of scriptural example and support.) Baptism relates to your commitment because it tends to happen shortly after your commitment takes place and because it is another step in the discipleship process. It is a testimony to others of what God has done for you, an outward sign of an inward work. As you participate in the baptism process, you are literally saying by your actions to those who are looking on, "Jesus has come into my heart and forgiven me of my sins."

This is an emotional event for some people and a powerful one for most. So if you have brought some of your unsaved friends to the baptism, it can be a great opportunity for God to speak to their hearts as well, a time of great testimony for you. This, I highly recommend; be sure to plan your baptism with your pastor in advance so you can bring friends and family. This unusual opportunity for witness, at a place where there will be other Christians available for prayer and help, is one that should not be missed!

I recall a baptism where I was helping a local pastor baptize several new converts I had been discipling. I was working in his church as an associate at the time and had worked to lead some of the relatives of these new converts to the Lord, with differing degrees of success. At this baptismal service, as a certain man, wife, and the wife's sister were baptized, the second husband sitting in the congregation felt completely left behind and was drawn to the Lord. As the minister gave a brief opportunity at the end of the service for anyone to come forward for prayer, this husband did and was saved. As it turned out, though, he was the only unsaved person in the church that day! What a loss! He had strongly resisted God and was an influential leader of his peers and family. If others had been there that day, perhaps many would have been saved!

Except for this testimony, the reaffirmation of your commitment you will probably experience in doing it, and the spiritual seal of the Holy Spirit, baptism itself does nothing to relieve us of sin. There is nothing special about the water or, as some say, in its value to wash away your sins; it is simply a symbolic testimony of your faith in Jesus Christ. In the Great Commission given to the disciples in Matthew 28:19–20 (KJV), Jesus says, "Go and teach all nations, baptizing them," and thus we receive our command to be baptized. Jesus Himself and many other followers were baptized by John the Baptist (Mark 1:9–11). The disciples baptized their new converts, and the great apostle Paul baptized his new converts, and the command continues to us today.

There are at least three common methods of practicing baptism, and they are as follows: (1) Sprinkling—this is where the hand of the minister is dipped into a bowl or other container of water, and then the water is flicked onto the head and body of the recipient; (2) Pouring—this is where the water is usually in an ornate container like a pitcher or flask, and then the minister pours the water over the head of the recipient; (3) Immersion—this is where a recipient is usually standing in the water with the minister and a helper and is then actually dipped or dunked under the water completely. This method obviously requires a different setup or location than the other two and is usually done in a baptistery (an almost hot-tub type of facility built into the church) or in an outside location, such as a pond or large stream. Some Christians believe that this method should be the only one practiced as it is most like the baptisms of the Bible. However, that is not practical for all people, nor preferential for many people, nor a biblical requirement; hence, any method sincerely done can meet the requirement of the Bible and have the same impact on believer and onlooker. Remember, it is what Jesus has done for you in your heart (inward work) that is important! Baptism is simply the testimony (outward sign) of that work done in your heart. I hope that your baptism is a powerful one and is an impact on your unsaved friends and family. Be sure to invite them to the event and to pray in advance that God will speak to their hearts.

Begin to Live Christlike

What does it mean to be Christian? Let's explore a little. What does it mean to be a "Buckeye" or to be a "Trojan?" Doesn't it mean to be of Ohio, or Ohio State, and of USC? Of course, and to be Christian means to be of Christ. Then to be of something seems to mean to have similar words, actions, thoughts, patterns, likes, etc., of the original. Like being a fan of Ohio State or of USC, so to be Christ-like is to be of the original—to be like Christ.

Jesus wants us to be Christ-like. We were created originally in the image and likeness of God (Genesis 1:26), and you, remember, went far astray, starting with Adam and Eve. So as we become Christians, we begin the long road back in becoming Christ-like again.

Now, just as an Ohio State or USC freshman learns what is expected of them as they start into college and become a real fan of their perspective university, a new Christian also begins the learning process. Christ does not, for instance, expect you to immediately act as if you have been a Christian for ten years. It is a slowly built process of learning who Christ is and taking on His characteristics. Always remember that He is the pattern!

That does not mean that you can emulate the life and pattern of someone who is an older Christian and always be Christ-like. You must be careful not to follow the wrong pattern. "Study to show thy self approved unto God, a workman that needeth not be ashamed, rightly dividing the word of truth" (2 Timothy 2:15, KJV), and "[W]ork out your own salvation with fear and trembling" (Philippians 2:12, KJV) are scriptures that make you ultimately responsible for your own position with Christ. You obviously must trust someone, and you should; but read, study, and look at the wide patterns of Christianity rather than one or two individuals. Paul says in 1 Thessalonians 5:20–21 (KJV), "Do not despise prophetic utterances (preaching) but examine everything carefully; hold fast to that which is good." The indication here is that there may, at times, be "that which is bad" that you do not want to hold on to. This is wise scriptural advice and should be followed; Jesus must always be used as the pattern.

I encourage you to begin the process of living like Christ! Study the scriptures and the lives of great Christians of the past and find out what Christ is really like. What attitudes does Christ display? How would Christ act if in such and such a situation?

Would Christ go here or there? These are the questions that you want to ask yourself. And slowly, as you learn more and more about Christ, you will gradually take on His characteristics if you are sincere about this Christian walk. Do not be discouraged if the process is slow. Jesus will be satisfied if your attitude is sincere and walk is consistent. You do not have to be "Mr. Fast Christian."

The Bible details for us many characteristics of Christ that we can pattern ourselves after. It is impossible, for instance, to look much at the New Testament without seeing the compassion of Jesus. While here on Earth as a human, He would spend long hours healing and ministering to the needs of people. His love for mankind is perhaps His most outstanding trait. It drove Him to suffer life as a human, be beaten and abused, and to die for a lost world. His integrity in dealing with the Pharisees is well known; His resistance against temptation and sin, perfect; His sharing of the Living Water, of Himself, and His peace in the storm are qualities we all desire. These and many more are qualities that you can begin to incorporate into your life. Slowly, as you study the life of Jesus, you will, with sincere heart, begin to look, act, and be like Jesus.

In this process of study and practice, your goal should be to become a mini-Christ (Matthew 5:14). Not with His power and divine presence, but in letting others see Jesus Christ in you for the purpose of sharing the Gospel of Jesus. It is us that Christ uses in this world to spread the Gospel. Unless we have a burden to share and win, like Jesus did for us, many of our friends and loved ones will not come to know Jesus as a personal Savior. You may be the only person in their world who can show to them Christ.

Depend Upon God

The last topic of this chapter, as you begin your new walk with Jesus, is about you depending upon God in every area of your life. Remember all things come from God (John 1:1–3). He is the

One who can supply for your every need (Philippines 4:19) and desire (Mark 11:24) if He pleases. He is the Everlasting Father, the Creator, Wisdom, and Love.

God brought you to where you are today. Without Him, you certainly would not be a Christian or be in the position you are in at this time. He knows what you need, when you need it, how and where you need it (Matthew 6:24–34) even before you ask; trust Him! His Spirit has drawn you to Himself; you are dependent upon Him whether you realize it or not.

This, I think, is the "Grand Paradox" of the Bible: God created us to be the mostly independent, self-sufficient persons we are, needing little from anyone. However, as we come to know Him more deeply, He says to us, "Depend upon me." It is not always easy to learn to depend upon God. Keep this in the forefront of your mind. Practice it every day. Pray about the most common of everyday situations, asking God to help you with them. Then as you come across the more difficult problems in life, it will be easier to ask God for His help then.

Jesus will never fail you (Deuteronomy 31:6, Joshua 1:5)! Never! Sometimes, we back away from Him, and He is not there when we need Him because of our actions, but He will not forsake you. If you can learn now to trust and depend upon God, you will have found a trustworthy friend for life! The old song says, "What a friend we have in Jesus, all our sins and grief's to bear. What a privilege to carry, everything to God in prayer. Oh, what peace we often forfeit, Oh, what needless pain we bear, all because we do not carry, everything to God in prayer." Trust Him, new Christian, and you will never regret it!

2

Prayer

"And when you pray, do not be like the hypocrites, for they love to pray standing in the synagogues and on the street corners to be seen by men. I tell you the truth, they have received their reward in full. But when you pray, go into your room, close the door and pray to your Father, who is unseen. Then your Father, who sees what is done in secret, will reward you. And when you pray, do not keep on babbling like pagans, for they think they will be heard because of their many words. Do not be like them, for your Father knows what you need before you ask Him."
Jesus speaking as recorded by Matthew in Matthew 6:5–8 (KJV)

Prayer

Okay, new Christian, how's your prayer life? Have you found it difficult to converse with someone who you cannot see, feel, or audibly hear? Are your prayers very brief and mostly made up of request? Do you feel that your prayers only go about as high as your head? Do days go by when you find that you haven't prayed? Are you trying to have a serious prayer life in the car while you travel from place to place? Do your mealtime prayers make up the bulk of your prayer time with God? Let's talk about prayer.

Prayer: Who and What

First of all, I think it critical to remember we are, while in prayer, conversing with a living being. God is not some figment of our imagination. He is not an it or a stone figurine. He is the Creator-God of the Universe. He can talk back to us. He does not want to be treated as a bust of George Washington.

Secondly, He requires of us that we do not have this God-man relationship with any other being—real or imagined. We are to have no other gods before Him (Exodus 20:1–3). He alone is the Creator-God who deserves the two-way relationship with us. God loves us very much! Yes, you! Regardless of who you are or what you have done, God loves you. He may disdain and even hate what you have done or what you stand for, but He still loves you. He desires of you a relationship, partially through prayer, where the two of you can get to know each other very well and where you will grow to love Him very much also.

As a matter of fact, as we become a Christian, God's love reaches out to us in a different and even more meaningful way. The Hebrew writer tells us in Hebrews 4:14–16 (Nasv) that once we become a Christian, "we do not have a high priest who cannot sympathize with our weaknesses, but one who has been tempted in all things as we are." This means not only does Jesus care about us, but He has gone through the same things that we are going through; He understands us completely, and He is sympathetic to our difficulties. In the Gospels, (Matthew, Mark, Luke and John) Jesus says, ask and seek and knock, and we will find what we are after. In James (kjv), the writer says, "If any man lack wisdom, let him ask of God, who gives liberally."

So then, these verses say to us concerning prayer, Jesus wants to converse with us about what we are facing and going through. He wants us to come to Him with our problems and to discuss them with Him, the Creator-God of the Universe, and with only Him as the Higher Power. That is done through prayer.

Conversation

Prayer is a two-way conversation. It is for the purpose of you talking to God and for Him talking to you. One of the quickest ways to ruin any relationship, as you probably well know, is to have no communication. This is not an option for any serious Christian; it is an absolute must! And it is just like any human relationship. It is to discuss the small unimportant items as well as the heavyweight decisions; the weather as well as the marriage plans; and the vacation as well as the buying of a house. Jesus is interested in you and your life. If you are involved or interacting in a situation, then Jesus is as well; He will discuss it with you. (Later in this book, we will discuss just how to know God's will in a given situation.)

This conversation you are having with God is not just a request line. This is not "Saturday Night at the Oldies." Certainly, God is interested in your request and wants to give you good gifts (Matthew 7:7–11), but that is not all He is interested in. He wants to know your feelings and your hurts, your thoughts and your desires, and your love for Him. He wants to hear your praise of Him; your thanks for His good gift of love; your adoration of who He is. These things might come strange at first, but you will come to enjoy these times as much as God does if you really love Him. Remember again that God originally created mankind that He might have someone to love Him voluntarily; He wants that love. Also, remember He is a being and needs and desires your love. And know that He will respond to your love with love and kindness of His own!

Are you married? If not, do you know of a good marriage? Compare that marriage with this relationship between you and God in the area of conversation and communication. How necessary is good communication in that marriage? How much do those people in that marital relationship desire to be loved? How much do those people in that marital relationship liked to be stroked and praised? In that sense, you get an idea of the importance of this communication with God.

Prayer: When

Prayer is not only an absolute, but it is an everyday absolute! Again, compare that marital relationship with this prayer life. If you or whoever got up in the morning and said nothing to your wife or husband—not through your bathroom routine, not through your breakfast, not throughout the day from work, not through dinner and the evening that followed, nothing—how long would it really have taken for your spouse to demand a response and an answer to your silence? My guess is in a loving relationship, you would never have gotten through breakfast. Should God and His loving relationship be any different?

You can and should pray any time and indeed all the time. In 1 Thessalonians 5:17 (KJV), Paul urges us to "pray without ceasing." We can literally stay in an attitude of prayer all the time if necessary. We can pray short prayers, little pieces of conversation throughout our day regardless of what we are doing. We can schedule short times of prayer early in the morning, on our breaks, at lunch, in the evening, or whenever we have a few moments to get alone with God. Prayer, or this conversation with God, should go on, on an ongoing basis throughout the day, just as if you had your spouse or good friend with you all the time. Most of us talk to our spouses nowadays throughout the day with the much-expanded cell phone access. Our spouses would think something wrong if we did not take their calls. You do have God with you all the time. Does He wait for us because we do not take His calls?

You should also have a specific time each day to get alone with God for several minutes or half an hour, just you and Him. This is your private time of prayer, again, just as you might spend some time alone with a spouse or good friend. This should be a specifically scheduled time each day as much as is possible. It is time for you and God to draw close to each other (James 4:8). Included in this time could be a time of quiet meditation—you listening to God. A common mistake of many new and older Christians alike is to talk to God without giving Him a chance to talk back to them. Don't make this mistake; take time to listen to God.

As your relationship deepens with God, your time alone with Him will lengthen. You will spend more time both talking and listening. Another common mistake of many Christians is to say "I have quality time with God" (or spouse or family) even though I don't have quantity time to spend. Let me say there is no such thing with God! Perhaps there is quality in that emergency prayer, "Lord, help me now!" but there is not quality in much else that short. He should be the highest priority of your life; therefore, you should make time for your relationship with Him. *You will not find depth of relationship with God until you spend time alone with God.*

Crises are again times when prayer is an absolute. These times are sometimes difficult, times in which to gain an understanding of spirituality, so these situations represent times when it is critical to get alone with God. Let's say, for instance, that you or a family member is very sick. This is sometimes difficult for a Christian to accept when we serve a God with all power. But we do not always have a firm understanding of God's will. He may allow us to process through such a time in order to draw us closer than we might otherwise be motivated to allow, at that time. So during such times, we must be very aware of God and His conversation with us. We must be very careful to get alone with Him and both talk and listen.

Preparation times represent another important time for us to get alone with God. If we are preparing for teaching a Sunday-School class, preparing for work, preparing for a vacation, preparing for marriage, or preparing for whatever, we will need God's guidance and leadership. Since God is omniscient (all knowing) and since He tells us to approach Him for wisdom, these preparation times are perfect times to ask God to give us of Himself. What greater power could we possible tap into? What greater advantage could we possibly desire? How better to prepare ourselves than to be led of God's Spirit?

Thankful times are also times worth mentioning about being in prayer. God, you remember, is a being like you and me, and He likes to be thanked for things He does for us. Remember always to give proper credit to man and to God. The Bible says that He inhabits our praise and that all good things come down from the Father of Lights (James 1:17). Don't forget to be thankful.

Prayer: Where

Prayer is something that can literally be offered up to God from anywhere! You can pray on the bus, on the plane, in the hospital, or in the store, or you can pray in your bed, on the couch, or on the toilet. It can be alone, with a person or two, or in a massive crowd. God is also omnipresent (everywhere at once), so He can hear you from anywhere. However, prayer from some of these places may not be as desirable as from others.

Again, I think it is important for you to regularly get alone with God. There are some things I'm sure you would rather not discuss with the whole church that you may well want to talk to God about. Alone is the place. Scripture tells us in Matthew 6:5–8, we should pray in our private closet of prayer where only God sees us, and then He will reward us openly in the final reward. Jesus obviously prayed many times in the presence of other people; however, for any major time of stress (before He was tempted in Matthew 4:1–3, before He chose the twelve disciples in Luke 6:12–16, after a very busy or draining time in Mark 6:30–46, and before His arrest and crucifixion in Matthew 26:36–50), He got alone to talk with His Heavenly Father. You should cultivate regularly scheduled times alone with God.

Also, concentration is important. When you are trying to pray but instead are daydreaming about a golf game, a speedboat, or a beautiful horse, you will not have effective communication with Almighty God. That is a little like talking to your boss about a problem that you are having on the job while he is talking on the phone with someone else. That is not only ineffective but disrespectful.

One more point about being alone with God–intimacy. Again, let me say that you will never find depth of relationship with God until you have spent time alone with God. Let's go back to the comparison of the marriage or the close personal relationship. When does that relationship cultivate deep loving feelings, a close love bond between two people? At the zoo with five thousand other people? An important time perhaps, but not for cultivating the feelings that we are discussing. These feelings may be generated at the zoo or elsewhere, but the relationship bond is sealed as we spend time alone with each other. Jesus said the greatest commandment was, "Thou shall love the Lord thy God with all thy heart, and with all thy soul, and with all thy mind" (Matthew 22:37, KJV). Although this commandment is probably more to be practiced than to be prayed, this place with God is never realized without intense concentration while we are spending some time alone with Him.

On a more practical note, body positions from which we pray can be very important if they affect the quality of our prayer life.

Some would have us believe that one can only approach God on bended knee. This is a very effective position from which to pray for more than one reason: as we kneel in prayer, many times, we humble ourselves before God as we do at no other time. God is due this respect. This humility, then, many times brings about an honest outpouring of our hearts, which makes for very effective praying. But it can also be effective for us to walk, to stand, to sit, or to lay down.

Comfort or discomfort of a certain position may be the deciding factor. As we have already spoken briefly about, to daydream or to dream because we have fallen asleep while praying is not appropriate treatment of God or effective praying. We are human, and there will be times when sleep overtakes our best intentions, and I believe God understands those times; but again, a close personal relationship with God is developed through time spent alone with God. We must manage to be awake! Do what you must do to be awake as you pray! (This is a great reason for having your major prayer time early in the morning.) How would it affect your relationship with husband/wife or boyfriend/girlfriend if you fell asleep while having an intimate phone conversation? So if it means you have to sit, stand, pray out loud, or walk while you pray, so be it. Pray from a position that you can concentrate from and from which you can be comfortably awake.

One thing that might help in this process of concentration and is a concern for where we pray (so we can write) and can help form a very effective prayer life is a prayer journal. This can work in many ways to help you be an "effectual, fervent" (James 5:16, KJV) person of prayer. This journal, for instance, should contain your active prayer list. This is a listing of the people and situations that you are lifting to God on a regular basis. This should be a changing, ever-evolving list as prayers are answered and God shows you direction about situations. In this journal, you may want to write out a condensed prayer. This allows for specific praying, for reviewing the thrust of your prayer effort, and for a concentrated mind while praying. You may want to pour out your feelings to God here by listing how you feel about a situation or person. By dating the entries in a journal, there is no mistake about the last time that you were in serious conversation with God. And there is room here for you to develop your own style and use for a prayer journal. The journal itself, however, can be a great asset to your prayer life.

Prayer: How

Just as with other things, there are ways of praying that are more effective than others. Many people might think or say here, "What method? Talking to God is talking to God." But if we compare this to roller-skating, for instance, some would say, "Anyone can get on a pair of skates," and that is probably true. Certainly though, no one would deny that some people can skate a great deal better than can others; squatting, backward, jumping, on one skate, with great speed—you get the picture. And then there is me. I have never been on a roller rink floor in my entire life! My style would be the guy getting his fingers run over by the jumper or the person skating backward! With praying also, there are some guidelines about how to pray that can make you a great deal more effective. A simple "Hello God" most anyone may be able to do. *Effective, relationship-building* conversation with God takes, at least, some serious effort.

Sincerity

As was discussed in chapter one about the Christian life as a whole, sincerity in praying is a key that you cannot afford to ever overlook. It is apparent throughout the history of mankind; God is a serious Being and is interested in us being serious when in conversation with Him. (I don't believe this means God does not have a sense of humor, but that is a different line of thought.) God has taught us not to treat Him in a casual manner but to reverence and to respect Him. When Moses addressed God in the burning bush, God instructed Moses to remove his shoes as a symbol of reverence (Exodus 3:1–6). God commands in the third commandment we do not take His name in vain, meaning that we not use His name thoughtlessly or carelessly (Exodus 20:7). When the ark of the covenant was moved in (1 Chronicles 13:6–14) and proper care was not taken to prevent its toppling over, it was touched by a priest to steady it, and he was struck dead as God had warned of in advance. God wants us to be sincere with Him. We show great disrespect when we make God an accessory to our day and don't give Him proper sincerity of attitude. God, on the other hand, will respond to what we feel in our heart. When something means a great deal to us, we will show sincerity, and it will mean a great deal to God.

James tells us that "the effectual, fervent prayer of a righteous man avails much" (KJV), and this fervency is closely tied to sincerity but speaks to the degree of our feelings about the particular subject. For instance, we can be sincere about wanting the school to pick up our kids when we send them out in the morning for school, but I'm sure you could become fervent in your desire to have them picked up if you see the bus driver drive by your house and forget them. You might race out of the house, waving your arms and saying, "Hey, hey, you forgot my kids!" That is more than sincerity; that's fervency. When you get that desirous of God, He listens more carefully, and responds more carefully. Again, when something means a great deal to us, we will show sincerity, and even fervency, and it will pull harder on the heartstrings of God.

Because of all this, (listen carefully) you become the most effective person of prayer about people and needs closest to your heart. Your family and close friends, who you care the most about, can naturally be the people you are most sincere about, even fervent. You are now, perhaps, the only person or prayer between those you care about and the fires of hell. That should make you very sincere! This does not mean you are responsible for their souls; they are responsible! It just makes you responsible to pray hard for them! Help give them all the advantage they can possibly have! All this does not mean that you should not pray for your pastor, your church family, missions around the world, etc., but it does give to you a responsibility for those close to you that you have not had before.

Faith/Belief/Trust

The next key to effective praying is simple faith. You have already exhibited faith in that you trusted God to forgive you and save you, so you do have faith in God. This is somewhat like the ability to pray, which we discussed at the top of this section; almost anyone can show some faith. And it does not take a great deal of faith to move God to answer seemingly huge prayers. Matthew 17:20 says faith the size of a grain of mustard seed (very tiny) can move mountains. Faith in God allowed Abraham, at age one hundred, and his wife, Sarah, at age ninety, to conceive and give birth to their first child (Genesis 17:15–19). God allowed Moses in faith to divide the Red Sea and for him and the children of Israel to walk across on dry ground (Exodus 14:21–22). Faith in God allowed Peter to walk on top of the water like Christ (Matthew 14:22–33). What can you do for God by exercising your faith? Simply believing and trusting God to act is faith. Despite the odds against you, despite those that don't believe, despite the critical nature of the situation or how hard the devil may be fighting against you, God can and will act if you have faith. (Because of the importance of faith, we will cover it more fully in the next chapter that deals only with faith.)

Scriptural Power: Prayer Promises

The last item that I want to cover in this section is what I call "prayer formulas." First, though, remember there are no shortcuts to effectiveness with God. It will take a concentrated effort on your part to survive spiritually and to be useful to God's kingdom. Secondly, then, it seems God has naturally put together some scriptures that can help us to be better people of prayer and to know that we are moving in the right direction. (Listen carefully.) When considering scripture about any particular subject and evaluating what God is saying about that subject, all scripture about that subject must be considered in order to get a correct view. So one cannot just pull out one verse from scripture and say, "This idea is exclusively correct." For instance, pulling out scriptures at random one could say, "He went out and hanged Himself; go ye and do likewise" (Matthew 27:5, Judges 7:17). That is an incorrect view of scripture. So, you see, that careful deliberation about what the whole of scripture really says about a given topic is important. So again, with any given single scripture or set of verses about prayer, one must be careful when pulling them out alone, that an injustice is not done to the whole of what

God is saying about the topic of prayer. So then finally, a prayer formula is a scripture or set of verses that is compact in nature, complete in itself, yet flows together, giving powerful access to God and yet does not do injustice to the whole of what God says about prayer. These formulas work as any formula might, in that one strings together the different points of the formula in the right order in an effort to find the desired results. The key thing about prayer formulas is that when we meet the criteria of the formula, God seems to guarantee the result. Let's look at a couple of examples:

a. Psalms 1:1–3

These first three verses of the Psalms seem to lend themselves in the direction of a life formula. I mean by that, if one lives as the initial verses instruct, God seems to promise blessing almost in blanket fashion. Borrowing from G. Campbell Morgan on *Notes on the Psalms*, verse 1 seems to progress in a direction away from the world and toward God. "Happy is the man who does not take the wicked for his guide, nor walk the road that sinners tread, nor take his seat among the scornful" (NEB). Morgan explains that this stand then walk then sit is a movement toward sinfulness. He says that these verses show either a general movement away from God (stand, with, walk, with, sit, with) or a general movement toward God (delight in the law of the Lord with mediation day and night). Verse 2 then continues the same line of thought but with a direction toward God. "The law of the Lord is his delight, the law his meditation night and day" (NEB). This continues the direction toward God by spending time in the Word of God and in meditation about God's precepts. It also reflects one's heart as this process is His "delight." Now God has already said that this person is happy or blessed because of their life's direction, but then the scripture continues to extend the blessing. Verse 3 says this person will be one who has a continual source of power for living, who will produce the fruits of a good life, and this power and good life will not "wither" away. Then comes the blanket promise. Consider, of course, that this person is doing all the above and would not have desires outside God's will for Himself, but the promise is strong and all encompassing. "[I]n all that he does he prospers" (NEB). What an outstanding promise from God! What a way to live one's life! This is a formula.

b. John 9:31 and 1 John 5:14–15

Again, these three verses seem to combine in a way so as not to violate scriptural integrity about prayer and yet to create great power and expectation in prayer. The verse in John 9 speaks to who God will and will not hear in prayer. "Now we know that God hears not sinners" (KJV), speaks, of course, to the prayer process going on in the situation being discussed in the context of chapter 9. This man who has been healed is referring to the fact that Jesus healed him through the process of drawing on God the Father for power. He is, therefore, classifying Jesus as a non-sinner because God responded to Him with the power necessary to heal. He seems to be drawing upon Psalms 66:18, where David says (paraphrased), "If I know there is sin in my heart, God will not listen to me pray." This does not mean that God will not hear the prayer of a sinner asking for forgiveness. It does mean God chooses not to hear a sinner who might call on Him to act in any other given situation. The verse continues, "But if any man be a worshiper of God, and doeth His will, him He hears" (KJV). So this first part of the formula indicates to us that in order for us to expect God to hear us, (1) we must not be a sinner, (2) we must worship God, (3) and we must do the will of God. With each of these points could be attached a great deal of explanation, but for now, I will leave that to your conscience. We continue, then, with 1 John 5, and it adds one more point about God hearing us. "And this is the confidence that we have in Him, that, if we ask anything according to His will, He hears us" (KJV). So, (4), we must ask according to God's will. If we are unsure of what God's will is, then using this prayer formula may require some preparation time. Once again, though, when the formula is met, we get an almost-blanket promise. Verse 15 (KJV) continues, "And if we know that He hear us, whatsoever we ask, we know that we have the petitions that we desired of Him." Think of that promise! Whatever we ask inside the confines of the formula, He promises to us, in advance! If you can pray from a position like this, you can pray from a position of great power and confidence.

These are natural scriptural formulas for our benefit in living and in prayer. They are not shortcuts to the good life! God looks on the heart and reads your very innermost thoughts and feelings. He is looking for that "fervent prayer of a righteous man" (KJV), and He knows when He hears it. Use these, and others that you may discover, for boldness and confidence in going before God in prayer.

Prayer: Why

There are many "small" (of course with God, there are no small reasons) and daily reasons to be given for going to God in prayer. The list could be endless. I want, however, to deal with what I hope are three very significant reasons for you as a new Christian. Again, these are perhaps not the three most significant reasons and may not seem even particularly important to some of you, but I think if you are serious about God, these will fit into what you are trying to do.

a. James 4:8a. I know that we have touched already on this passage, however, it is one of those standout portions of scripture that can be and do great things for us as Christians (even as non-Christians). This is a promise from God. It is without strings or attached requirements. It does not reflect any degree of response on our part, or God's part. Paraphrased, it simply means, "Move toward God, and He will move toward you!" Imagine how you can do this through prayer. As you pour out your heart to God and describe to Him your day, your hurt, your desire to see a loved one saved, or your desire for Him to meet a need for you, He begins to empathize with you and to feel for you, and a bond between you begins to build. You are drawing close to Him, and He is responding. He leads you to do a particular thing; you do it. He asks you to witness; you obey and do it. He convinces you to help a needy family; you do as He asks and show His love to the family. He leads you to a teaching ministry in your Sunday school; you respond by teaching and living the love of God into the lives of eight-year-old kids, let's say. In all this, you constantly move toward God. What does He do? That's exactly right; He moves toward you, and the two of you become closer and closer.

This is a very powerful dynamic that will work for you over and over or on a constant basis and is an excellent reason why you should pray!

b. The next reason is really best illustrated by the process of human greed and desire for power. One of the best places to view those human emotions in action is corporate America or, perhaps, Wall Street.

Certainly, not all people in business or on Wall Street are greedy, power-hungry money grubbers, but many are, and Wall Street is synonymous with the type. It is that type or those base desires that I want to point to here. Because whether we like to admit it or not, all of us have some of that type of emotion in us unless God has purged it all out. At some point in your life, you have wondered what it would be like to have all the power that money can buy. We all know the feeling of being recognized from the front, "Hey, I have connections!" How about the feeling of making a weighty decision and everyone else in the family agrees? We all like to say, "My so and so works for the mayor or the governor." You recognize what I am talking about. All of us like to be, at least, tied into the power. Now stop and think about this feeling in relation to prayer. God is the power of the universe! He is power! God can do anything! Speaking of having connections! Just pause a moment and reflect on that; God is all power, and you are His son or daughter. Of course, He does not allow us to abuse or squander His power on our own ambitions and desires, but if our purpose in life is to do the will of God, to please God, then you are directly connected to the Power Source! You have access to more power than you can ever use! Prayer is your connection with the Power Source.

c. Accomplishing something for God is usually a desire of most new Christians. To see my point here, try to picture the reverse of the last point. God is the source of all power, so without being connected to Him, you have *no* power. It is that simple; if you want to accomplish anything for God, you will have to stay connected to God through prayer (John 15).

Last week, (at original writing, now sometime ago)I had the privilege of meeting one of God's old warriors. Kenneth Harting is ninety-eight years old. I don't know how or when or why he learned the lesson of this point, but I realized while hearing Him pray one day that he knew he must stay connected to God. I was leaving his home, and he wanted to have prayer together before I left. As we stood in his living room with some others who were there, he prayed, and I heard the following statement, "We just need your help, God. Even if we are just doing nothing God, we need your help." The statement was not "in anything we do, we need your help," it was, "even when we are not doing anything, we need God's help." How true that is! The Power Source is God; you will accomplish nothing, less than nothing, without His help!

Why pray? Draw close to God, and He will draw close to you, and prayer is a great way to do that. Secondly, prayer is the connector that you have to the Power Source of the universe. And without that connection and His help, you will never do anything for the kingdom of God.

One last note on prayer in this chapter.

Pray specific prayers, and you will get specific answers. (Let that sink in.) Many times, Christians get discouraged because they think that God is not answering their prayers. But if we pray, "God help me today," He will, but you will probably not know when it happens. He will have helped you stay out of an accident, have helped soothe your emotions, or have helped you find something you lost, but will have done so in an unobtrusive manner that you did not recognize. And then you become discouraged, thinking that God does not answer your prayers. So if you want specific answers that you can recognize, pray specific prayers!

3

Faith

"And what is faith? Faith gives substance
to our hopes, and makes us
certain of realities we do not see. It is
for their faith that the men of
old stand on record."
—Hebrews 11:1–2 (NEB)

Faith

Definitions

As we have already discussed faith in a small measure in the last chapter and because you have had life experience, you already have some basic idea of the definition of faith. Faith, of course, translates into trust and belief, but it is sometimes an elusive element to pin down. To define faith, we will look in several directions in order to gain a well-rounded perspective. Let's start with the *Funk and Wagnall's Standard Dictionary*.

Funk and Wagnall states (1) belief without evidence; (2) confidence or dependence on a person, statement, or thing as trustworthy; (3) belief in God. All of these are faith, and that's why, perhaps, sometimes we are a little unsure of just what is meant by the faith we are reading or hearing about. Let's look at each of them but in reverse Funk and Wagnall order. In this study, of course, remember we are looking at these definitions in the light of discipleship or following after God.

A. (3) Belief in God.

Faith is then, first of all, acceptance of the fact God does exist. Despite the fact you have never seen God, you have never touched God, and many say that God does not exist, you believe in God. How? By simple trust or belief God is who He says He is in His Word—by faith. God does not offer proofs on demand of His existence but rather ask us to accept Him by faith (Matthew 12:38–40). There are, of course, many evidences God does exist. Look at the order of the universe; how each planet, star, and moon has their own order, their own function in the total universe. How delicately each of those things intertwine, and yet they have never been out of place. Do we really believe a random cosmic explosion threw all these things into place by mere chance? Look at the intricacies of the human body: the brain, the nervous system, the muscles, ligaments, and tendons, the function of the organs and yards and yards of blood vessels, the breathing-air-interchange system, and the immune and protection systems. Do we really believe that we *just* evolved from tadpoles? How about the times God has spoken to your heart? Was that just your imagination? Was it your imagination that brought about the change in your heart and life? All these are evidences offered by God. Faith in God is to accept all this and believe that God is. This is Funk and Wagnall's number 3—belief in God.

B. (2) Confidence or dependence upon a person, statement or thing as trustworthy

This is the most common usage of the word *faith* to most of us. We put trust in our car to take us to Florida for vacation because it, or a car like it, has done it before. We learn to trust our mates, our children, our dogs, our freezers, our furnaces, our neighbors, our friends, and their word, etc.; this is a process. We try it again and again and learn to trust because he, she, or it does not let us down. We tend to think of this more as earned trust than a faith.

Where God is concerned, we build up a trust just as with our neighbors. We pray, God answers, and a trust is built. Over a period of days, months, and years of our lives, God never lets us down, and we learn to rely on Him. We learn to trust His Word. We trust His presence. We trust His reactions. We trust His promises. Therefore, confidence in a person as trustworthy.

C. 1) Belief without evidence

This is a hard one! To trust or believe without the benefit of prior experience, without any evidence that it will turn out like you want. This hard one is what you are asked to embrace as a new Christian. Without prior experience with God, you are asked to trust Him to forgive your sins. You are asked to trust Him to give you eternal life. You are asked to trust Him to keep your soul from eternal hell! You are asked to trust in His Word. This is a difficult process for some people. It has been described as a "leap of faith," almost like jumping off a cliff. That leap is rewarded, of course, because God never fails, but we are asked to accept that also. Some time then, as we continue to walk with God, we ask Him for something, and then we must just trust Him without any evidence that it will really be the way you are praying. That is the true meaning of faith where discipleship is concerned—the Bible says "childlike" faith.

When my wife was a child, her father was not well for many years. He loved his children, his wife, and his God, but he was sick for a long time also. This did not always work the best in building security into his little girl because she knew he was not well and could not take care of her. One day, at about age seven for her, thinking her daddy had gone to the basement, she headed down the steps to check out what he was up to. As she reached the landing about halfway down, they spied each other, and he turned toward her and held out his arms. "Jump, Lainey. Jump!" he said. "Jump, Lainey. Jump!" Could she trust him? Would he catch her? These questions raced through her mind. Then she jumped, and he caught her. And he said, "Jump into the arms of Jesus, Lainey, and He will never fail you!" What a powerful lesson for a seven-year-old child or for you! That is what Jesus is asking of you! Jump and trust Him!

Lastly, then, we find a definition of faith in the Bible itself. In Hebrews 11:1 (NIV), we read, "Now faith is being sure of what we hope for and certain of what we do not see." This definition is a compilation of the technical dictionary definitions at which we have already looked. "Being sure of what we hope for" could be part of both the number 2 and number 3 definitions. We might be trusting God for a response for the first time, or we might be trusting for a response from God after having done the very same thing before—different types of faith. Or in "certain of what we do not see," we find number 3, faith in God, although we cannot see Him. So in the Bible or in our study of faith, we might find ourselves discussing different types of faith but all called faith. Whether it is trust in the fact that God exist, faith in God to act, faith in the reliability of God's Word (the Bible), or whatever the technical definition, we equate it as reliance upon God. It's all faith! Let's try to further understand faith as we look at different facts about faith.

Another element in the attitude of faith is the key component of anticipatory waiting. That is a fancy way to say that when we are exercising our faith with a request, we need to expect God to act upon our faith. A part of successful faith is the element of asking with the expectation of receiving from God (Matthew 8:5–10 and 15:21–28).

When in high school, I attended the private boarding school in Jackson, Kentucky, Mount Carmel High School. It was a school founded and run, at that time, by Miss. Lela G. McConnel, entirely by faith. It was inexpensive to attend, making it available even to the underprivileged mountain children.

Miss. McConnel felt called of God to minister and, as such, did not operate from a "this world strong" financial base. The teachers and staff volunteered their time and expertise with the understanding if money came into the school in excess of the monthly operational budget, they would then receive some income that month. On this basis, over the two and a half years I spent there, I witnessed several times when the school was in desperate need of some operational cash and witnessed the money literally being "prayed in." I saw times when Miss. McConnel would come into our morning chapel and share that the school had some specific financial need and then lead in prayer, asking God to supply the need. Then as God was looking ahead to her request and the mail having run while we were in chapel, I have seen her leave chapel and go to the mailbox and return praising God for the immediate answer to her request. That act of going to the mailbox looking for the immediate answer to her prayer is the expectation to which I am referring. You will have to work at the process of exercising faith to that degree; that usually takes some time and practice, which many times means desperate situations. But God wants us to expect Him to act!

God may not always choose to answer your prayers in such an immediate fashion, but if you are meeting the other requirements of prayer we have discussed (God in your heart, worshipper of God, in God's will, etc.), then you should always expect an answer from God!

Hearing that story, you might think answers to prayers like Miss McConnel's require a great deal of faith, more faith than you have or might ever have. That is exactly what the devil wants you to think! However, it is just not true according to the Bible. In Matthew 17:20, Jesus is teaching His disciples about how much faith it takes to perform great miracles. You can see by reading there His indication is that it only takes faith the size of a mustard seed (about this * big) to cause God to act in a great way! You *now* have that much faith! Sure you do! You believe in God, don't you? And He has saved you from your sins, hasn't He? See there. You had faith, and God acted!

In Matthew 14:28–31 is the story of Peter stepping out of a boat and walking on water to meet Jesus. As he is doing this, he becomes afraid, doubts God, and begins to sink. Obviously from this and from other scriptures about Peter at this time of his life, he was not a strong believer. Yet in the beginning of his walk, he had sufficient faith to walk on water! It does not take huge amounts of faith to get God to respond to our request. *You can receive answers to your prayers!*

History

The Bible, secular history, and the current lives of Christians are full of stories about how God has rewarded faith in Himself. This subject has made up hundreds of books in itself. There is an almost-endless supply of material to read in this category, so we will only look at a very, very few samples for our purposes here.

If you were raised in Sunday school or have seen the movie, you know the story of the children of Israel fleeing from the Egyptians and encountering the Red Sea as an obstacle. As the approximately one to four million Israelis piled up against the edge of the water, Pharaoh and the army of Egypt bore down on them from behind. Pharaoh had changed his mind about letting his slaves go free. Moses consulted God and followed instructions. As he raised his staff and stretched it out over the water, God divided the sea with a strong wind, pushing the water back on both sides and allowing the Israelis to cross on dry land. At the same time, God held back the approaching army with a wall of fire. Later, as the Egyptians tried the same crossing, the water roared back into place and destroyed them. Moses's faith in God had brought about a miracle (Exodus 14).

Another such incident happening in the Old Testament to a later leader involved Joshua. On this day, Israel was fighting the Amorites over the land, which God had given to Israel. There were many Amorites, so after some great deal of fighting, God even poured down hailstones from heaven onto the Amorites, killing more than even the Israelis has killed. However, there were still many Amorites on the battlefield to contend with, so Joshua commanded the sun to stand still so they could have continued sunlit hours in which to do battle. And it did! God rewarded Joshua's faith, and for the length of time of about one day, the scripture says, "[T]he Lord listened to the voice of a man" (NASB) and the sun and the moon stood still and Israel was successful (Joshua 10).

As we move forward in scripture into the New Testament, we see many miracles of faith, which surrounded Jesus's ministry. Jesus was walking along one day and was approached by a centurion, a Roman army officer in charge of about a hundred soldiers. The centurion was worried about a servant of his who had become paralyzed with palsy. Jesus quickly said He would go to the servant. But the officer, in an act of great faith, simply requested of Jesus to speak the word, saying he was not worthy of a visit of Jesus to his home. He believed in Jesus's authority over sickness and believed his servant would be healed. Jesus marveled at the faith of this non-Jewish soldier, and the servant was immediately made whole (Matthew 8:5–13).

In an attempt at one time to help people exercise their faith in Him, at least in His power to work miracles, Jesus allowed a good friend of His to die while He stayed away. Then a few days later, when He went to the area where Lazarus lived, there were many mourners and family members there. After sharing briefly with the family and weeping with them, Jesus followed the group to the gravesite and instructed the gravestone be rolled away. After praying a short audible prayer for God the Father to help those watching to believe on Jesus as the Son of God, Jesus called Lazarus from the dead. This is a story of Jesus's power, not a story of great faith, but was meant by Jesus to cultivate faith in Him (John 11:1–46). With this in mind, I remind you of another statement of Jesus's. In John 14:12 (NEB), Jesus says, "In truth, in the very truth, I tell you, He that has faith in Me will do what I am doing; and he will do greater things still because I am going to the Father." Faith is the key.

Recalling a story from my childhood, I remember hearing John Nobel speak. He was a Christian who had escaped Communist Russia when the government tried to put him to death. He told the story of some other Christians being put to an agonizing death for their belief in God. The Russians soldiers had marched the four or five Christians to the edge of a frozen lake in the dead of the Russian winter. Once there, they built a huge roaring fire to keep themselves warm, made the Christians undress, and marched them out onto the ice. If the Christians would recant their faith in God, the soldiers said, they would be welcomed back to their clothes and the fire. And they waited. As it became dark, the Christians stood on the ice and sang hymns to God. Finally, however, one Christian man recanted and made his way back to the fire. As he dressed and began to warm himself by the fire, one of the soldiers began to undress. When questioned, he said he had seen a halo around the head of the Christian and was taking his place and embracing belief in God! That was true faith!

One last story of modern day faith. In the late '70s and early '80s, I pastored a small church in Westland, Michigan. When I went there as pastor, the church had a small Ford bus they had owned for about six years but had never used for Sunday school. Toward the middle of my first year there, we decided to attempt a bus ministry to children and readied the bus for use. We cleaned it up, replaced a few bad parts, and obtained a driver and workers from the congregation. We planned, then, a Saturday when many of us were to go out into a housing project and try to round up as many kids as possible for a great start. The night before that start Saturday, I became very sick with a bad fever. On Saturday, when all of us were supposed to be at the housing project, I was in bed, and no one went on visitation. As I lay in bed that day, contemplating the situation, God spoke to me and clearly showed me my sickness was an effort on the part of the devil to defeat our bus ministry. I reaffirmed in my heart and mind God's will and determined Westland, Michigan, would have the bus ministry God wanted.

When I was well, we began the process of beginning again. A new date was set and announced, and people recruited for the big push. Then a problem was discovered. The Ford bus, which had been fine, was now not running.

The story becomes incredible at this point and moves straight into Ephesians 6. There we read in verse 12 (KJV), "For we wrestle not against flesh and blood, but against principalities, against powers, against the rulers of the darkness of this world." For the next year, we and professional mechanics did everything in our power to find the problem, fix, and return the bus to running order. As I recall this story and as I have consulted with others who lived it, there was hardly a week that passed that someone was not doing something to that bus. Maybe in the course of that year, a couple or three weeks of holidays went by without work going on. To portray the idea that constant work and attempts to start that bus went on for a year is not an exaggeration. We found problems we did not know existed. Problems that had nothing to do with the bus not running, but we fixed them as we combed over the bus. We fixed, adjusted, and/or replaced the alternator, the battery, the starter, the carburetor (rebuilt in and out of the shop about four times), the tappets, the brake lines, the spark plugs and wires, the coil, filters, oil, vacuum lines, etc. We pulled that bus, pushed it, jumped it, and charged it. I remember once glancing out my front picture window at the parsonage and seeing the bus fly past the house. I thought, "Someone got the bus started!" As I went to the door and looked out, though, I saw the long cable running to a big four-wheel-drive truck that was towing the bus as the bus driver tried in vain to start the bus by popping the clutch. We tried everything! But the bus would not run!

One Sunday, as I preached about faith in God, I challenged the people God was capable of anything and we should not limit Him to our small thoughts. Unexpectedly, someone spoke up from the congregation at that moment and challenged me by saying, "Pastor, if what you are saying is true, we should be able to ask God to start our bus and it happen!" My heart pounded, and I admit for a moment I could see myself pulling my foot out of my mouth. But I responded as God wanted me to respond and said to them, "You are exactly right, and we should. How many of you would be interested in going into the church parking lot after church and praying for the bus?"

After church, we did just that. Many people would not participate and stood near the church building watching. A number of us, however, gathered around the front of the bus and began to pray. We told God about all we had done to start the bus, as if He did not know. We reminded God this bus ministry was His idea in the first place, as if He did not know that too. And we ask God to start the bus, claiming God's promises as we prayed. Then the bus driver, a young man in his early twenties, John Nye, stepped forward and got into the bus. He turned the engine over once, twice, and on the third try, it started! I have lost track of the bus now some years later, but that bus ran for years without a hitch! Through our faith in God, the power of the devil had been broken, and our bus ministry began. That bus ministry was very successful, winning many children and adults to the Lord and training others into ministry. That very first bus captain, Joe Stafford, was later called into ministry and to this day is the pastor of a church in Ohio.

As I reedit this chapter some time after the original writing, I am reminded again how much God did through the bus ministry in Westland. Over a number of years after I had left that church as pastor, my younger brother who had moved there, married, and stayed in Westland for some time, would occasionally call me and say, "Hey, Mike, remember such and such a family or person from the old bus route?" He would proceed to tell me about someone getting saved or, once, about numbers of family members from one family who came to Christ during a revival time from the old original route. No wonder the devil fought hard to keep the process from starting! Faith had been exercised, God's will done, and dividends were paid spiritually for years afterward.

Developing Our Faith

Faith, even mustard-seed-sized faith, can simply be there in a person's life; you might just trust God out of a trusting personality or background. However, you might not have such a background or, worse yet, have a very suspicious personality or a background cultivating a lack of trust. Depending upon how you have been reared as a child, depending upon your experiences with father figures in your life (God is a father type), or maybe just because of your style of operation at this stage of your life, you might have to develop a working faith in God. This is entirely in order, and even biblical. In Mark 9:14–24 (KJV), one person responded to Jesus's question about believing with, "Yes, I believe; but help my unbelief." They were struggling to believe and still had some doubt in their heart. Jesus understands and helps us build our faith. This process is much like any building process; it happens over a period of time and involves a series of efforts.

For instance, it could be compared to a dating relationship. It begins with the courage to ask someone out on a simple "scratch the surface kind" of outing: coffee, lunch, something at work with other persons involved—something safe. Then the dating relationship slowly, or not so slowly, progresses to dinner, dinner and a movie, the zoo, and so on to a candlelight dinner for two at the Lord Fox restaurant. You know the routine. Slowly, we risk more and more of our emotions and learn to trust the other person with our innermost feelings. Developing faith is much the same. We begin to trust God and ask God for simple things:

His help throughout the day, His help when we are sick, for Him to help someone we know. Slowly, as we converse with Him and learn to know Him better, we trust Him more and more. Soon we are sharing our innermost feelings and asking Him for leadership, which we believe we cannot do without. Soon we trust Him with our children, our lives, our future, our everything.

In Malachi (Mal-la-kai), an Old Testament book written by a prophet of God, we are challenged by God to live our lives in such a way we exhibit total faith in God. If we do, God promises, in Malachi, to pour out blessings upon us in such abundance we will not be able to receive all of them. What a challenge! If we can step up to the challenge of living our lives in such a way we are exhibiting total faith in God, we begin to live within the "grand paradox" of the Bible. Let me explain. God has made humans in such a way we are basically self-sufficient. Then God asks us to depend upon Him. This is sometimes very hard to do, but it is the life of faith. What a paradoxical situation!

In Matthew 6:19–34, Jesus is teaching about trusting one master—about faith—and He uses wildlife as a tool of comparison. Look at the birds and the flowers. They do not work for a living or to feed themselves or work to make their clothing. But Jesus says, "I take care of them." Then He challenges us. "Don't worry about tomorrow. You can't do anything about it anyway! Instead, seek first the kingdom of God and His righteousness and I, God, will give you all of those earthly things you need. I already know you need those things" (loosely paraphrased). *This is the challenge of faith for each of us!* Can you turn your life over to God and allow Him to provide while you seek His will and His way first?

We will talk more of this in a later book in this series, but there is such a thing as a spiritual gift of faith. But this kind of faith is within someone whose spiritual gift is faith. (Every Christian is given at least one spiritual gift from God the Holy Spirit.) A spiritual gift is some area of a person's life that is particularly empowered by God to do for God! A person with the spiritual gift of faith is a person who can trust God for the very difficult issues or situations or for very "big" answers to prayer. This is someone who can give to God the opportunity to speak to others through their uncommon belief in Him. This gives God a billboard others can see. Maybe you have that kind of faith; maybe not. Regardless, you have some measure of faith! Build on it! Trust God! Use it or likely lose it!

New Convert, I don't know what God has in mind for your future or what obstacles you might encounter in your walk with God, but I do know God is bigger and more capable than any "principality, power, ruler of darkness, or spiritual host of wickedness" (Ephesians 6, NKJV) you will ever encounter! Jesus states in Matthew 28:18 (NKJV), "[A]ll authority (power) has been given to Me in heaven and on earth." New Convert, you can tap into that power by exercising your faith! That is a powerful thought! *Always respect the level of hate the devil has for God because you can get in the way, but always remember as long as your heart belongs to God, any amount of faith in God can defeat the devil!*

4

Sharing Your God

"I pray that you may be active in sharing your
faith, so that you will have a full understanding
of every good thing we have in Christ."
—Philemon 6 (NIV)

Sharing Your God

Sharing God! Sounds scary! "I'm not sure I want to do that," or "I'm sure I do not want to do that!" If your reaction is something like that, you're certainly not alone. All of us, at one time or another, have had that response! But hang on! It's really not that bad. Please read on.

Introduction

Let's first start with what sharing God is not. All of us have had misconceptions about what sharing God really means, and the devil has used those misunderstandings against us. When this happens, God's work does not move forward.

Sharing God is not going door-to-door nonstop trying to win every neighbor you have. It's not being so fully focused on your testimony you cannot speak to people about anything else! It's not standing on a street corner shouting the Word of God to passersby. Even though each of the above examples could be legitimate if so led by God, these are not the norm and not what we are dealing with here. Also, the Bible and studies of the church show us only about 10 percent of Christians have a gift of evangelizing others. So we are also not talking here about the concentration of ministry someone might have!

In this chapter, we are dealing with every Christian's obligation to share Christ when the time is right and when God has opened the door. These are people to whom God will give you a desire to minister. From your position as a new Christian, many things about the Christian life probably seem difficult and strange. However, as in this situation, Christ only expects output from us as we come to understand His desires *and* are prepared and empowered by Him to accomplish these things. In that light, we need not fear this new task because God will give us the power and the ability to do His will, all in His time. Don't be scared away by the lies of the devil as he attempts to separate you from God! God has been faithful to bring you this far and is well capable of supplying all your needs as you push toward more knowledge about Him and His will. God promises in His Word not to allow us to be stuck out there beyond His help (1 Corinthians 10:13; 1 Thessalonians 5:24). This means God will not require any task of you until you are equipped to accomplish it, and when a difficult task is requested, He has the grace, meaning help (Philippians 4:19), necessary to allow you to complete His request. Trust Him; Jesus will never fail you!

God's Command

In Matthew 28:19–20 (NKJV), Jesus says in part, "All authority has been given to Me in heaven and on earth. Go, therefore, and make disciples of all the nations, baptizing them in the name of the Father and of the Son and of the Holy Spirit, teaching them to observe all things that I have commanded you; and lo, I am with you always, even to the end of the age." Historically, this command was given to the disciples after Christ rose from the dead but is also given to the church as a whole and not meant for just a few people. It encompasses each of us in its scope. But even if we have a ministry from God to a foreign country, we still wouldn't literally fulfill this scripture. No one can go to all the nations; this is a command to a group—the Christian church as a whole. Most of us live out the meaning of this scripture where we are. "Making disciples…and teaching them to observe," simply put, is telling people when God opens the door or telling them what He did for them on the cross. This allows God to speak to them and creates an opportunity for them to accept Him. The opportunity to actually lead someone to Christ will not nearly always be yours, but you will have participated in the process by your testimony or witness. Acts 1:8 goes on to promise us the power of the Holy Spirit and challenges us to start witnessing near home then to spread out from there. Remember the disciples of Jesus were challenged to reach the world with the gospel. Their job was to establish a church that would eventually reach the world. The church would continue to witness, train, and spread God's word! All of Jesus's disciples lost their lives in this process. Because the established church and the various governments of Jesus's day did not want to lose creditability and power, they persecuted and killed the disciples. But through the power of the same Spirit Jesus promises to us, the fire of Christianity was set ablaze, never to be extinguished. It still burns today, and God will give you power and ability to witness at the right time.

Over in John 15, Jesus likens us to branches that sprout off the main vine (Jesus). He states, like with the grapevine, we, the branches, have no power of our own to produce, but He wants us to produce. He says we can get our needed power from Him, the Vine. He explains, if we produce through His power, the Father will still prune us or test us so we might grow stronger, producing even more. Jesus also says if we do not produce through His power, we will be cut off from the Vine and burned in the fire, just like unproductive grape branches. Three main points: (1) Jesus asks us to produce, all of us; (2) He does not expect us to do this alone. He not only promises us the power to do so but also clearly says we cannot produce without His power; and (3) He says we will be cut off if we do not produce. Sounds scary again, doesn't it? Not really. Jesus is like the father who requires us to mow the lawn. Then He goes out and buys a riding mower, a trim mower, an edger, and a weed eater. Then He comes out each time and helps us do the job and pays us for doing it! It really is not as bad as it sounds! God gives us all the tools; He comes in the power of the Holy Spirit and helps us do the job, then He promises us eternal rewards when we get to heaven! Really, not too bad!

In God's plan of salvation for the world, He works through humans most every time He can. God can work supernaturally and does, but most often, He works His will and plan through you and me. Then since His will is for no one to be lost but instead come to Him (John 3:16–17), He needs all of the yous and mes He can get out there telling others about His love. In this way of using the "human" plan, the gospel has spread from those first few disciples to other devoted followers of Jesus, to the day of Pentecost written of in Acts 2, to the known world of that day, to Europe, and on to those of us in America, as our forefathers sought religious freedoms, and on to most other parts of the world. We have many to be thankful of who have come before us, and we have a responsibility to our loved ones and those who will come after us to do our part! God's plan of salvation is functioning in the world today! Now you are going to become a part of this worldwide eternal plan (Ephesians 2:19–22).

What Others Do (Or Not Do)

This is a critical area where you must keep your eyes upon Christ and His example. Remember it is Christ, who is the Son of God, and His Word we are trying to obey. As we have just read, this is of importance to the entire world! What you do in this area of witness may affect scores, thousands, or even millions of people as God continues to use the "human" plan to spread the gospel.

Many examples can be cited about individuals—Sunday-school teachers, neighbors, boy or girl scout leaders, foster parents, even unknowns who someone sat beside on a plane or train—who have changed the course of history for thousands of others by witnessing to a single person. It was a shoe salesman who witnessed to D. L. Moody and led him to the Lord. D. L. Moody went on to become one of the most outstanding evangelist of the early 1900s and won thousands to the Lord Himself. But beyond that, someone has traced the path of convert and influence from D. L. Moody eventually to Dr. Billy Graham, who has also won thousands, perhaps millions, to Christ. Look at the impact, even if partial, of that one faithful shoe salesman! This is a critical area where we just cannot know the full impact of our involvement! Every single time we witness, there is the potential of worldwide impact!

Because of this, we cannot afford to watch other Christians and what they are or are not doing. Many Christians are lethargic or lazy and do not witness. We do not want to judge them here or want you to do so later. That's not our job. Please leave that to the Lord Himself. However, do not follow their example either. Again, you must keep your eyes upon Christ. It is the tendency for new Christians to conform to the spiritual or "Christian" lifestyle pattern of other Christians around them. *That can be fatal!* Remember, branches that do not produce are cut off and burned! Many people today believing they are Christians, are in the church, and doing some things within the church, will be a part of Christ's harsh judgment spoken of in Matthew 25:31–46. You cannot get caught up in looking, watching, and becoming like other Christians.

In Acts 3:1–11 (NIV), a story is told of the healing of a lame man by God through Peter and John. In verse 5, we read, "So the man gave them his attention, expecting to get something from them." He did not get what he expected since he was begging and wanted some money, but he was expecting to receive something!

I am convinced the world around us is still expecting to receive something from us! We have the answers for which the culture is looking. Certainly God needs you and me to do our parts in the overall picture of worldwide evangelism. We cannot be Tom-like, Bob-like, or like Mike; we must be Christlike!

How to Share

There are various ways of sharing the gospel with other people. We will look at three: testimony, witness, and referral. It's not so bad. Take a deep breath. Don't let the devil scare you away. Remember God has already won this war! We are participating in battle skirmishes, and the scars of spiritual warfare are a beautiful thing (Matthew 5:10–12 and Galatians 6.17).

When God opens the door for you to share, most of the time, it is the easiest to simply tell what God has done for you. You may be having lunch with someone or talking over the back fence. You may be at work, on the ball field, or in a store. Wherever you are, whatever you are doing, you will recognize the opportunity as presented by God. God will make the opportunity available, and you will know. That first time especially, your heart will pound, you may have a lump in your throat, or you may even break out in a sweat. But if you will overcome those human obstacles, you will receive a tremendous blessing from God. You are about to pass on the secret to life—eternal life! You are about to impact an eternal soul toward Christ. By just telling a person about your experience with Christ, about your change in life, you become a part of helping them toward Christ. Remember, God does not expect anything from you He does not inform you of, and He does not empower you to do. Remember also, you are the branch and you have no ability to produce without the power of the Vine. This is a team effort! You are the human agent. The power of God the Father working through the death and spilled blood of His son Jesus and through the presence of the Holy Spirit all working within you, are now reaching out to this person to whom you are about to testify. How can you go wrong? How can you possibility fail? God says His Word is sharper than any double-edged sword, knifing into man's conscience and that it will not return to him without effect (Hebrews 4:12, Isaiah 55:11). If you can use any scripture (John 3:16) in telling your story, think of its impact! Think of the thoughts and words you share that the Holy Spirit will now have opportunity to use as He draws this person toward Jesus. This is a win-win situation. Regardless of what the immediate outcome is, you have completed a part of your responsibility in the worldwide outreach of the church for God.

I have been using the words *witness* and *testify* interchangeably; however, they are slightly different. To testify in this sense is really to tell about you, about what God has done for you. To witness slides over into telling about them, about what God can do for them. There is obvious overlap between the two. Some of what God has done for you is also what God can do for them. That is why it is effective to tell others what God has done for you. Witnessing, then, is the second way we can share our God.

You must be a little more careful about how you witness or just exactly how you word your witness. It is reasonable, but not absolutely necessary, to go out with an older Christian a few times. Listen to them witness in order to get a feel for this process. There are points about witnessing you will want to be familiar with before you begin. For instance, normally, one goal in sharing with others is not to be inflammatory. We know from Jesus's example that sometimes inflammatory happens or is necessary, but I encourage you as a new Christian to steer clear of these situations. These instances, if necessary at all, are tricky business and for those with much more experience. So one must be careful in how you phrase your witness so as not to offend the person you are trying to help. They obviously must realize that sin is present in their lives and their need for Christ. That imprinting of need upon their heart is the job of the Holy Spirit, not your job! Our job is to share the good news of the gospel. Even if you feel this person has never darkened the door of a church, you must be careful. Christ does not want us to judge or to push people away from Him.

When we talk to people about having sin in their lives, it is opportunity for them to feel singled out and to feel like we are saying they are not good people. This is why we need to be so careful. One way to avoid hurting people is perhaps to give them opportunity to ask questions. A pause, waiting for them to respond, or even asking, "What do you think?" may open the door for you to carry the conversation even further. In this way, *they* get to introduce the topic or area of discussion without feeling you are intruding or pushing too hard. But even if they ask about what sins they may have in their life, be general (Romans 6:23) and gentle, and allow the Holy Spirit to do His work. If you point out specific things you think they may doing wrong, even if you are right, it may be too soon for them to accept. It's not wrong for you to say, even about obvious sins, "It's not for me to judge you. Allow the Holy Spirit of God to speak to you about that," or to refer them to a scripture you know of that speaks about their question. In this way, God gets to speak to them directly from His Word. If done in love and carefulness, this will be God speaking to them, not you accusing them. You might read the scripture or let them read the scripture and then ask, "Does that speak to your question?" Again, the goal is to help, not hurt! Common sense here goes a long way. How would you have wanted to be treated while you were still in sin?

There are other scriptures and questions and conversational methods to use when witnessing so someone. Generally, you will want to steer normal conversation toward spiritual things gradually. Then lead them toward questions, scriptures, your testimony, etc., in an effort to lead them to Christ. Two mainstays of witnessing then would be a greater use of scripture and giving them the opportunity to pray and accept Christ into their heart.

Knowing a few scriptures well enough, being sensitive to the Holy Spirit in a way to know when to offer the opportunity to pray, knowing the answers to some common questions, are all important to witnessing and come with time, study, practice, and spiritual maturity. As a brand-new Christian, I encourage you to work with more mature Christians in developing your witnessing technique. For now, while you study and grow spiritually, you can testify (tell your story) and use the third method of sharing Christ.

For our discussion here, the third way of sharing Christ is to make a referral. Once you have had discussion with this person you are trying to reach and are at a place where you are uncomfortable, take the person to your pastor or to a mature Christian who can continue the process. Your testimony is still the most effective part, and they will know how to bring the process to closure with an acceptance prayer. This is perfectly normal and correct. Would you want your doctor to treat you past the point of his or her expertise or to refer you to a specialist? Remember, the goal here is to help and to win the person to Christ if possible, not to score personal points. God will know perfectly well your involvement and will reward you; leave that to Him. If in the time with the person you are trying to help, you have been honest and caring and you have won their confidence, they will probably allow you to lead them to the "specialist." Stay with them if you can, and they will feel better about it, and you will learn from the "specialist." In the future, then, you will be able to lead people to Christ on your own. This is all a part of the new-Christian process.

Motivation to Share

Can you even imagine the total impact that Christ's love has had on your life? Can you even begin to comprehend what life would be like if Christ had not come to earth and died as a sacrifice for our sins? I know my life would have been grossly different without Christ! I came to Jesus and became a Christian at a very early age, following the example of my parents. I grew up in a Christian home with both parents serving God in legitimate fashion. I had the privilege of weekly Sunday school, vacation Bible school, revivals, camp meetings, church youth camps, family devotions, godly friends, Christian reading materials, and my father teaching us biblical doctrine each week. Without all this, I can't imagine where life might have taken me. I still grew up with a nasty temper. It alone could have cost me my life. I did not know proper boundaries of teasing, and it almost cost me my life more than once! Only God's love and mercy has given me the desire and will power to follow Him. Only God's patience has put up with me over and over again! I owe Christ everything! And all this says nothing of the promise of eternal life! This indebtedness motivates me to love and obey Christ.

Of course, we cannot buy eternal salvation, and we can never repay Christ for His boundless love and grace toward us! But shouldn't we be motivated to give Him all we can? Shouldn't we be motivated to follow His Word as closely as possible? Shouldn't His example of giving teach us to give back to Him and to others? Remember the picture of Christianity is God reaching down to mankind, not man trying to reach up to God and appease Him. In following Christ's example, then, we too should reach out to all mankind and be givers like Christ. Let God's love for you, and conversely, your love for Him, be a motivating factor in your sharing the good news of Jesus Christ.

As we discuss motivation, we need to see another debt each Christian has: someone shared with us! Where would any of us be unless Christians before us had been willing to share? They, no doubt, experienced the same hesitations you and I feel. They probably felt witnessing was not their personality. They were scared to share that first time. *But someone did, or you would not know Jesus today!*

When we look down the road, then, to generations beyond ourselves, will there be a line of people who never became Christians because we did not witness? I know a minister friend of mine who, after years of bi-vocational ministry (driving truck and pastoring), recently retired from the truck driving just a couple of years short of full retirement. As we spoke about it, he told me he took half the amount of retirement he could have had if he had just waited two or three more years. When I questioned his decision, he said this, "God showed me two groups of people. These on the left were the ones I had and would win to Him in my lifetime. There was an even bigger crowd on the right, and I ask God, 'Who are these?'" God said to him, "These are those who will not make it to heaven if you do not retire now!" Whoa, you say, that is heavy! Suddenly the devil begins to tell us we do not want this obligation or responsibility. This is too much. But again, remember we are talking about God opening the door for us and being the power behind making it all happen. We must trust the Lord! Don't let the devil derail you here! Remember the devil is a liar and the father of all lies! Forget what he says; resist him, and scripture says, he will flee from you. Your children, the children of your family and friends, your friends, neighbors, loved ones, and others need you to live the life in front of them and to share when God opens the door. You are now part of the worldwide process God is using to reach a lost world!

Also, for motivation, I think each Christian should try to gain a vision, a picture in their mind, of the "lostness" of the world. Ask God to help you with this picture. There are millions of souls who do not know about Christ as the Savior of the world. Think about how blessed we are to have intersected with someone who has prayed for and shared with us! Compare that with the number of people who have never even heard. The Bible says, "And how shall they hear without a preacher?" (Romans 10:14–15, ASV). In other words, how can the lost of the world possibly hear about Christ without someone to tell them? Someone who already knows. That's us! We should always be motivated to share because the world needs us!

Some years ago, a close missionary friend of mine died on the field in Papua New Guinea. They held a memorial service on the field and then brought her body home for a funeral at her home church. This was a difficult time for everyone: her husband, daughters, family, church, denomination, and more. Everyone gathered and went through the process, but at the funeral, I was blown away by one of the PNG nationals, a pastor. I guess there is a custom in this area of PNG where this missionary died, that if a person dies while visiting there, someone always accompanies the body back home. So this young pastor traveled to America with the body of the missionary as a representative of his people in order to keep the custom. He spoke at the funeral and began his remarks very professionally, "General superintendent, general missionary superintendent, general board, and general missionary board, family, and friends," and spotting in the crowd the original missionary to PNG to his area of the country even though that happened before his birth, he said with great respect, and to Don Seymour, the man who brought the Light of the Gospel to my valley..." It was as if nothing meant more to this man in the world than the opportunity to know Christ and then to respect the one who sacrificed to bring him the good news! We have an obligation to carry on God's plan and to share Jesus with all those to whom He opens the door!

As complex and scary as the devil tries to make this, the process is really just low-key, sharing with people where God opens the doors for us! It is critically important! It is the plan God put into place even before He created the world. It does reflect upon our caring and love for Christ. There are people out there who likely will not hear unless you do your part. "With man this is impossible; but with God all things are possible" (Matthew 19:26b, NIV). You can do this! I'm praying for your success!

5

Bible Study/Devotions

"Do your best to present yourself to God as one
approved, a workman who does not need to be ashamed
and who correctly handles the word of truth."
—2 Timothy 2:15 (NIV)

Bible Study / Devotions

To any serious follower of Christ, the study of His Word is a must. Like pouring over a map when hunting a lost treasure, the Christian who wants to claim the eternal treasure of heaven will spend time studying God's "Treasure Map." With the help of the Holy Spirit, the way is made clear within stories of Old Testament history and the prophets, and wrapped around New Testament history with the miracles and teachings of Christ.

Similarly, devotions (times of private worship) are critical to the process of the Christian walk. This is the time when we commune directly with the God of the Universe. This is the time when we allow God to speak to us. This is the time when we seek guidance for daily living, help for hurting emotions, love from the Master, and show love and caring back to Him. This is your private relationship with Jesus!

This chapter is about both of these times spent with Christ. And because God, you, and His Word are involved in both of these times, there is overlap and similarities between these different practices. This chapter, however, seeks to point out the differences between these two times spent with God for the sake of you getting the full benefit out of each of them. These can be exciting times as you learn about Jesus and the two of you build a strong relationship. They might also be times of discipline or rebuke as Jesus seeks to teach you His ways. They will certainly be times of learning if you give yourself to them in something more than a casual manner!

Let me caution you though; right here at the beginning, the devil does not wish you and God to share these times! He has a thousand ways and more to keep you from making this a part of your life. He will bring interruption after interruption; anything from dirty dishes and phone calls to serious crisis to thwart your efforts to draw close to God. You must make these times with God high priority! Don't allow anything to stand in the way of cultivating these times of spiritual growth and development! Probably, the devil will not quit brothering you after he sees you are very serious; he may well try to get in your way most of your life. After all, that is what he does. Remember, though, slowing you down or stopping you from reaching your full potential for God will not only affect you but your family, your friends and the people out there you don't even know right now who God has in your future. For the devil, this is heavyweight stuff; this is life or death. And so it is for you, new Christian, spiritual life or death.

As Christ did, rebuke the devil and the powers of darkness in Jesus's name! Simply, "Satan and powers of darkness, I rebuke you in Jesus name!" (These scriptures provide some insight: Zechariah 3:2, James 4:7, and Jude 8–9.) This is way deep stuff, and we will talk of this more later on, but it is effective because the devil must operate by the laws God set up for Him. In the book of Revelation, John tells of seeing saints in heaven around the throne of God and says they made it there "by the blood of the Lamb, and by the word of their testimony" (Revelation 12:11, KJV). Jesus's blood forgives our sins and grants us mercy and grace; your testimony is who you state you are and what you are going to do. To allow the powers of darkness to hear you say you are determined to live for God all your life is a powerful thing. Simply tell God your intentions and let Satan hear you! He may decide to work harder on someone less intent.

Many Christians start down this road with high aspirations and hopes, but before long, the devil slowly and carefully intertwines the "cares of this life" (Matthew 13:1–9, 18–23, KJV) into their lives, and all this draws them away from their time with God. If you are going to be a successful Christian, you will have to have a successful private life with Jesus. *Don't let the devil steal it away from you!* I cannot overemphasize this! These times, combined with your time of prayer, is your spiritual lifeline! If the devil is able to stop you, even significantly slow you down, you will begin to die spiritually. Depend upon God! *Be tough!*

Devotions

The word *devotion* has the following *Funk and Wagnall's Standard Dictionary* meanings: (1) the state of being devoted, as to religious faith or duty; (2) strong attachment or affection expressing itself in earnest service; (3) an act of worship or prayer. All these apply to the process of having *devotions*. Having a time of devotions comes from being *devoted* to Jesus Christ. The "strong attachment or affection" is what you will be seeking to build through this time of *worship* and *prayer*. Devotions then is a term coined by some Christians in the past, drawing all these dictionary meanings together. It is a mixture of all these meanings. Let's briefly discuss some of the varying parts of the mixture.

1. Prayer: this book contains a whole separate chapter on prayer. That's how important it is. Daily talking and listening to God is the only way to build a relationship. Prayer is the single most important aspect of the Christian's life! (Refer to chapter 2.)
2. Meditation: this also receives some coverage in chapter 2 but bears mentioning here. Devotions are a time of sharing.

As such, you need to give God opportunity to share with you. To sit, stand, walk, or however, but listening as God has opportunity to speak to you is a part of the devotional process. Listen and learn God's voice. He wants to commune with mankind (Deuteronomy 5:22–30). He may want to say how much He cares for you. He may want to challenge you. He may want to discipline you. He may want to say He loves you! You want to hear God's voice! This may be rather hard at the beginning because it is no longer fire and smoke, but give it time! God can, wants to, and will speak to you if you will listen.

3. Reading: the Bible is the most important way God speaks to each of us. Reading it through a chapter or two at a time is a great way to give Him that opportunity. God can bless, encourage, challenge, chastise, direct, compliment, and more through His Word. Read it regularly. Also other inspirational material, such as devotionals, Christian books, and magazines, can be helpful. You can learn from other's experiences and how they have been successful or what caused them to fail. All this helps you know the road ahead. However, nothing is more important than the Bible!

4. Singing: is a powerful tool of praise, of thanksgiving, and a reminder of God's love and ability to work in our lives. The Holy Spirit has inspired many Christian hymns and gospel songs. Especially if music is a favorite part of who you are, this can be a tool to teach, encourage, and charge you up to better serve the Master. During your time of devotions, you may want to sing to the Lord. Sing a verse of praise or a song of encouragement. Sing a song of commitment. Jesus is moved by sincere feelings of the heart and, many times, responds to our singing.

Devotions, then, are times of private worship! You should incorporate into your time spent with God whatever allows the two of you to communicate, whatever allows you to share your love with Jesus. Worship is showing your adoration, respect, humbleness, and love to Him, and then He in turn will bless you and show His love toward you. Sometimes, when times are hard, this time is spent showing Jesus your pain, frustration, or anger. That is good also. Jesus wants to share those times with you just as much. He has healing and help for those times. All this is two-way communication.

Take a practical approach to devotions. Remember they are times of high priority, but you do still have to exist in this world. You probably cannot have ten hours of devotions each day (of course, I'm exaggerating.) There would be nothing wrong with that, but if you work or have children, or even eat and sleep regularly, something more practical than ten hours a day still works well with Jesus. On the other hand, there is no such thing as a quality five minutes with God. Of course, this is actually untrue, except in the exact right circumstance, but let me use that statement to set up the following point. If you are shutting God out of your life to the point that there is only five minutes left for Him, He won't be there at all for very long! You will cut Him out completely. Find some practical time that allows you and God to communicate and still allows you to function in this world. Probably as a new Christian, fifteen to thirty minutes a day is a good start. Slowly, then, you will adjust this time into what helps you most each day.

Reading one, two, or three chapters a day should also be guided by what you can practically digest. The important thing is that you regularly, every day if humanly possible, commune with God. Spend enough time doing the things that work for you so you have spiritual strength and power to live successfully for Christ.

Bible Study

Personal Bible study is a little different. Although it can be time communing with God, it really is time to look into God's Word and learn about Him and the Christian walk. It's not just reading for devotional upliftment or encouragement for the day. This is time for a full meal of the meat of the Word (Hebrews 5:12–14, KJV). Paul here is speaking to Christians who should be grown to the point of a strong spiritual life. My reference to this verse, new Christian, is not about you, not yet being at that place; it speaks only to the fact there is growth like this, which is scripturally based and expected.

Why? Remember you are an "infant" Christian. Many of the characteristics of a human baby are correspondingly true of a spiritual infant. For instance, compare these: weakness, inexperience, lack of knowledge, the need for others to help, the need for frequent feedings, can only digest small amounts, and vulnerability. All these things correlate to infants and to new Christians. It is said little kids need help and special foods, and it can also be said that new Christians need the help of others and spiritual food so they can grow and become stronger and wiser about the ways of God. The study of God's Word is one of the best ways to grow and learn. It is critical to your survival process that you have keen interest in the things of God. This interest should motivate you to more study, prayer, and fellowship with other Christians. This is the growing process. When Jesus was leaving His disciples here on earth and going back to heaven, He told them He would send a Comforter who would, among other things, "teach you all things" (John 14:26, KJV). It is one of the duties of the Holy Spirit to teach us the things of God we don't understand. He is present when we study God's Word. He enlightens our minds and hearts. He allows us the ability to understand. You may be young and inexperienced, new Christian, but you have the best Teacher possible in the person of the Holy Spirit. Learning, then, should be an exciting process!

How? The Bible can be a scary place without some help early on. Not, of course, anything bad or wrong, but hard to understand. Probably one of the first moves for you is to get one of the newer versions of the Bible. This does not mean the doctrines or Jesus's words are new. It simply means the old English has been replaced with today's English. Also, it means the latest of biblical archeological discoveries have verified the text. Don't let this throw you! It simply means the textual discoveries of the last few hundred years, since the transcription and printing of the King James Version in 1611, have been reviewed and included. So old copying mistakes by a scribe or printing mistakes have been caught and updated back to the original. When different persons or printers all make copies of the same book over hundreds of years, whatever it is, mistakes will be made. Because different copies exist, though, comparisons and corrections can be made. These are not changes in the words of God or the stories of the Bible but corrections of man-made mistakes back to the original. So, then, the newer versions (NKJV, NIV, NASV, and others) have more modern language and are more easily understood. It does not help you to read anything you cannot understand. The language of 1611 is not easy to understand. The Kings James Version of the Bible is like reading old versions of Shakespeare—very hard to understand! Consult your pastor and get a version you can understand. What good is it to study anything if you cannot understand what you are reading?

Secondly, then use some guide like this book. Again, consult your pastor and get some material that will guide you through what you are studying. You can select from topics, books, people, time frames, doctrines, and even words to study in this way. Then whether by yourself, with another Christian, or in a class setting, you can delve into the "meat of the Word." Keep notes! Take your time! Pray over what you are studying! Compare it to other studies. Ask questions! Just like anywhere else, you will get out of this what you put into this. Certainly, the Holy Spirit will add His wisdom, but you will have to put forth your measure of effort. This is, though, a very rewarding effort. You will be learning about the God of heaven. You will be learning how to make heaven your eternal home. You will be learning how to take others with you. You will never study anything more important!

Later, after you grow some and become a little more mature, look into inductive study of God's Word. This is a method of study where you use only the Bible to study the Bible. You cross-reference verses, topics, and words. You depend upon the Holy Spirit even more to bring out the meaning of God's Word rather than depending upon someone else's interpretation. You study the Bible from the inside out, only checking yourself against outside sources once you have already drawn your own conclusions. This allows you to stay on track, and yet it will have the most meaning for you.

When? This question is hard to answer and, maybe in light of today's fast-paced society, even harder to accept on your part. I think some time of Bible study is worthwhile as often as you can, maybe every day. Do you work only once in a while? Do you eat only once every three days? You see my point? However, it is only worth it every day if you can give some appropriate amount of time and concentration to the study. If that is only every other day, every three days, or once a week, then so be it. But be *consistent* and *sincere* when you do study! Just going through the motions will not draw you closer to God. God looks on your heart. He knows the truth about how you approach this time of study. Study as regularly and as often as possible. Then try to screen out interruptions. Try to give thirty minutes to an hour of quality concentration and study each time. This will enhance your life with Christ more than I can even express. This will make you a leader for Christ in this world. Don't look on other's lives and say, "They are not doing this. Why should I?" This is an area where you must do what is right, whether anyone else is doing it or not! This is a dividing of the men from the boys, so to speak. This is an area of commitment that reminds me of the words of Christ in Revelation 3:15–16 (NKJV), "I know your works, that you are neither cold or hot. I could wish you were cold or hot. So then, because you are lukewarm, and neither cold or hot, I will vomit you out of my mouth." Many "Christians" fail God at this point of Bible study and allow themselves to become only lukewarm. This is not pleasing to God and, according to scripture, makes Him sick. This luke-warmness causes Christians to allow other things of this life to creep into their thoughts and actions. Sooner or later, this can have only one effect. They fall from grace, letting Christ slip away from them. This is not what you want. Study! Study regularly! Don't ever stop!

Where? Here is another practical evaluation. During your Bible study and devotions, you may encounter many emotions. You may want to cry, shout, dance, or talk out loud to God in expressing yourself. You may want to sing aloud. You want to be somewhere where you can experience these things without feeling limited. If you are home alone, no problem. If not, you probably want to find a place of privacy. As I have stated, you will want to be uninterrupted. You will certainly want to write. All these are considerations for you in deciding a place for Bible study and devotions. You do not want to lie down and then fall asleep. This only brings on feelings of guilt, and study is thwarted. Be practical in this approach. God will meet with you anywhere. You, however, may not be able to meet with God just anywhere and get study accomplished.

New Christian, I have and will continue to pray for your success!

6

Christian Associations

"They devoted themselves to the apostles' teaching and to the fellowship, to the breaking of bread and to prayer. Everyone was filled with awe, and many wonders and miraculous signs were done by the apostles. All the believers were together and had everything in common. Selling their possessions and goods, they gave to anyone as he had need. Every day they continued to meet together in the temple courts. They broke bread in their homes and ate together with glad and sincere hearts, praising God and enjoying the favor of all the people. And the Lord added to their number daily those who were being saved."
—Acts 2:42–47 (NIV)

Christian Associations

Introduction

This is an important and sensitive area of study. It may well be critical to your survival as a new Christian! There are no easy answers, and whatever answers are offered may well be controversial at best. Study this chapter in great detail with a prayerful heart and open mind to God. Nothing here is offered to offend or harm you; it's all offered in an effort to protect your soul from the devil and for you to find the way in which God can use you best to win your friends and family. Just as with your decision to accept Christ as Savior, the decisions of this chapter are yours. But know now, they are decisions with eternal implications! Allow what is written here to act as a guide and a help to you as you look to the Lord for guidance in this sensitive area of associations.

You Are Your Environment

In order for you to survive this new life you have started, it will be necessary for you to be careful of who and where you associate and to be in control during times when you are with non-Christian friends. The seriousness of this issue for you, new Christian, is illustrated by part of the judicial system of probation in our country. When someone convicted of a crime is finally let out of prison, one standard point of probation is that they are not allowed to associate with known criminals. Why is this? What does the old saying mean, "Birds of a feather flock together?" Why should we be careful of our associations?

In Psalm 1, we are challenged to move away from the world and move toward God. "Blessed is the man who walks not in the counsel of the ungodly, nor stands in the path of sinners, nor sits in the seat of the scornful" (Psalm 1:1, NKJV). G. Campbell Morgan explains this as a blessing for the person who shows a steady progress toward God and away from the world. He says the process of first walking with, standing with, then sitting with, demonstrates a progression of association away from God. Psalm 1:2 goes on then to say, "But (instead) his delight is in the law of the Lord, and in His law he meditates day and night" (Psalm 1:2, NKJV). This shows an opposite progression from verse 1, with one moving toward the things of God. This is what God wants us to do! This challenge of the psalmist is very fitting for the new Christian.

Old habits and ways die hard sometimes. This can be an area of difficulty for you, new Christian. The attraction of old haunts, friends, and habits can be the downfall of a new Christian's life. Not having many or any Christian friends yet leaves you hanging out there with no one but your non-Christian friends. This can tend to draw you back toward your non-Christian lifestyle. You must be willing to control your environment! You must be willing to put it all on the line if you are going to hang around some of your old friends. They need to know you have made a significant change in how you live. This does not have to be done in such a way to specifically make them feel guilty or put down. They just need to know you will be acting, talking, and doing differently.

This is not a statement you make to them unless they ask; this is in the doing and in your resolve. Saying it all to them puts them down. It's more in "I gave that up," or "No, thanks," or "Not any more, guys." In being around them, you accept them; in not participating in the wrong ways, you make a statement about you and God. In acting out your new lifestyle consistently is the only way to avoid your old wrongs and have a positive witness. In this way, most of the time, you can be in charge of what goes on around you. Then if you cannot control your friends, you can at least control yourself.

I have, for years, challenged my children, even when young, and the older ones on through their teen years, with this question when they were going to spend time with other people, "Who is in charge?" They have come to know that simple question is a reminder for them to control their environment concerning their physical and spiritual safety. They have come to know I will back them up in whatever way is necessary, if they become physically or spiritually uncomfortable with what is going on around them. God is saying something similar to you. He will be there for you if you will only let Him. It will be up to you to act to protect your new Christian status. Remember God will not force you to live for Him. He wants voluntary love. If you allow yourself into situations, conversations, places, or relationships that draw you away from God, He will not stop you by locking you in. The Lord will hurt for you. He will try to draw you back in the right direction. He will try to speak to you. He may send someone to try to reach out to you. Ultimately, you control your own environment. You control your own eternal future by the decisions you make.

None of this, however, says you cannot have non-Christian relationships! Indeed, God wants you to have those connections with the people of the world. How else does He have the opportunity through you to reach out to the lost people you know? He Himself was criticized by the church leaders of His day for hanging out with only poor people and sinners. But this brings about a difficult level of responsibility for one's own soul. You must be careful your motivations are right before God in wanting to be with those people, in those places, or in those relationships. That requires stark honesty with oneself.

There are also several areas that require prayer when considering these associations. What are the possible conflicts you may face? Will your non-Christian friends want to do things, go places, talk about topics, watch things, or otherwise be involved with things that will conflict with how you now feel or with how God feels about your involvement in those things? What would be the repercussion of your involvement? With you? With them? With others looking on? Will your non-Christian friends be doing things you have done before and become a temptation to you? Will giving into the temptation cause you to fail God? Will giving into the temptation cause your friends to disbelieve God's power? Are those temptations too great for you now? How can/will you have a witness with your friends without being with them? Will being a "goody two shoes" in their eyes turn your friends off? How can you appear to be the same old friend and yet manage to talk to them about spiritual things? How much do you talk to them about God without turning them off or away? Not a simple topic, is it? All of these and more are valuable considerations. In the next few pages, let's discuss some of these areas and hopefully find some guidelines.

Nature

If you now live a sincere Christian life and if you allow life to take you to the places and events of the Christian walk, you will slowly but surely draw away from your old friends because they will not automatically go along with you. This is a proven process among the Christian community that is both a blessing and a curse. Yes, Jesus wants you to associate with Christians (Acts 2:42–47 and Hebrews 10:21–25) for encouragement, growth, protection, and fellowship. That this draws you away from temptations and possible downfall is good. At the same time, the very action helping you mature as a Christian also draws you away from those who need your witness, and that is a negative. It's a tightrope to walk, but there are guidelines.

In Mark 8:36 (KJV), Jesus says, "For what is a man profited, if he shall gain the whole world and loses his own soul?" He is speaking here about financial matters, but we can draw some inference here also. Would, in this same light, it be correct to work so hard to win others to God but lose our own soul in the process? You might say, "Would God let that happen?" Remember we are our own environment; God will not force us to obey Him. Certainly there have been and are people who have gotten so wrapped up in doing good spiritual things they got sidetracked and lost out with God. So,

1. Others are very important, but our first spiritual priority is to our own soul. You will do no one any good if you lose out! As important as they are to God, all the souls in the world should not be as important as your own soul is to you. There are other areas where sacrifice for others is a quality desired, but not when considering your own soul. So we have traveled a long way to get to this point:
2. Ultimately, your friends are responsible for their own souls. Not that you do not play a role or have some responsibility; you do! But your own soul comes first!
3. You can only be a witness or be involved with your friends to the degree you do not damage your own soul. Now many times, this is not a factor, and you may struggle to understand this degree of caution. Sometimes this is critical, and others reading this book may not understand how it could be any other way. We all come to this point from differing backgrounds. Again, the evaluations and

choices are yours. An "old-time" measurement tool that is still of value today is to ask yourself this question:

4. "Would Jesus do this or say this or go here?" Yes, the old revived "What would Jesus do?" You should be trying to be a reflection of Christ. That is how your friends can come to know Him also. Even Jesus hanging out with the poor and the sinners did not mean He was doing wrong. He held to His standard.

5. You will not win your friends to Christ by lowering yourself to a sinful or near-sinful level. The picture of Christianity is God reaching down to mankind in order to lift Him up from a life of sin. When you become a Christian, you become a "new creature in Christ Jesus" (2 Corinthians 5:17). Don't look down your nose at your friends. Don't portray the idea you think you are better than they are in any way. But don't go back to an old lifestyle of sin just to try to stay on their good side either.

This process of becoming a useful tool for Christ in order to reach others is one that requires prayer, time, and some work. You need to mature, at least some, in order to recognize there are dangers out there. You need to develop some kind of prayer life because, regardless of what you do to win your friends, God the Holy Spirit must do His part! To know some scripture or to have a friend to call on is a great help as you talk to your non-Christian friends. Just to invite your friends to church or to a church event to meet some other Christian people is a valuable tool in this process. You do need to become aware of most of this as quickly as possible while you do still have those connections with non-Christian people. If possible, you need to establish yourself in positions where you have those connections, but do so being fully aware of the influence of the non-Christian world on you.

Reward/Defeat

This is possibly your time of greatest opportunity for winning your friends and family to Christ. They can see the changes in your life. They can see your enthusiasm for the things of God. They can feel the happiness and joy you now experience. As you pray for them, God the Holy Spirit uses these things and more to attract your friends to the God of the Universe whom you have embraced. During this time especially, pour out your heart to God, asking Him to influence your loved ones toward Him. Let God know your feelings. Let Him hear your fear about the eternal destination of the ones you love. Let Him feel the urgency within you about their salvation. Ask Him to convict and draw them toward Himself. Remember from chapter 2 where in James 5:16b (NKJV). The Bible says, "The effective, fervent prayer of a righteous person avails much." Effective prayer is prayer you feel. God responds to persons who feel deeply about what or who they are praying. This time as a new Christian is a time crucial to the winning of others around you. God wants to win your friends and family; be sure you do your part!

As we have talked about already, this is also the riskiest time for the possibility of losing one's salvation. The devil has many ways of drawing the new Christian away from God. Even the pressures of moving away from friends and family into a new lifestyle that may separate you from them is a valid tool for the devil. Expect Him to make the most of it. This will be something like a tug-of-war. You, with God's help, will be trying to pull your friends and family toward God, and the devil, trying also to use your friends and family, will be trying to pull you back. It is a life-and-death struggle well worth your every effort! Remember also nothing is more important—*nothing* more important—than your eternal soul. Everyone will spend eternity in either heaven or hell. Each one of us is responsible for our own choice. Pray for your loved ones. Cry for them. Beg God for them. Talk to them. Invite them. *But do not go to hell for them!*

Association Controls

What controls can you place upon yourself in order to protect yourself and yet have the most impact upon your loved ones? Are there things you can do that will cause this process to be successful for you? Certainly there are, and we will review some of them.

1. As I have been urging you, I will continue to say this is an issue to consult about with your pastor and/or spiritual mentor. Stay in touch with these people and in church throughout this critical time.
2. Practicing self-discipline is another way to keep you close to God. *Make* yourself do the things you know to be the right things: devotions, Bible study, church attendance, prayer times, etc. These things won't come easy at reunions, family picnics, ball games, camp outs and more, all on Sunday, just to keep you out of church and away from Christian people. The devil always has a plan. Do what is right for your soul. Work around these things. Go early or late or not at all to these non-church functions. The more you miss church, the easier it is to miss. It is not my specific goal here to separate you from your family and friends. On the contrary, I want you to keep in touch with the people you care most about! Just don't let the devil, through those people and functions, draw you away from God. Just as with any worthwhile endeavor, you will have to be self-disciplined to be successful here!
3. Set carefully thought-out limits in advance about places you will go, things you will do, language you will use or participate in, when you are hanging out with your friends. These limits should be set prayerfully and with pastoral discussion so to keep you from violating limits that will cost you spiritually. When you are flowing with

the excitement of the party or outing with your friends, this will provide you a boundary you do not have to think through on the spot. These will be flashing neon signs, reminding you of the value of your soul at a time when eternity is probably not the topic of discussion.

4. Then live by the limits!
5. In contrast to the negative limits, also set some positive goals you strive toward concerning these associations. When you know you will be spending time with non-Christian friends, have a time of prayer before you go to bolster your strength and faith. Pray for God to protect you, to give you strength, and to give you boldness to witness and wisdom as to when and how. You might be thinking, "I work with non-Christians every day!" Then early morning devotions are all the more important for you. Have a time of prayer when you are back home. Review your actions, thank God for helping you, and confess any failures. God knows how hard it is! Talk to Him about it all! Also set a goal about witnessing: when you will ask someone to church with you, when you will guide the discussion toward spiritual things, when you will bring some of your non-Christian friends together with some of your new Christian friends (party/golf/activity). Don't rush or force this process, but pray and ask God to guide you and to open the doors of possibility.
6. Don't forget to keep your non-Christian friends and family in constant prayer. Ask your Christian friends and church family to pray with you for their salvation. Be sincere with God.
7. Depend on God! God did make us basically self-sufficient but did also ask us to depend upon Him. Tell God about your weaknesses. Confess to God your need for His oversight, protection, wisdom, and help every day. Don't try to do this on your own. You alone are no match for

the devil. Only God has the power to help you overcome, especially when you are rubbing elbows with the world.
8. Be the leader, not the follower! Get your friends to go with you, listen to you, act like you. This is not to say you cannot have fun. Have fun, but clean wholesome fun! They will not always follow you. But as often as you can, be the leader slowly guiding them toward God.

I know some of this was repetitive. I have tried to cover this topic from several angles. Your eternal soul is at stake here. Try to make these suggestions work for you! Jesus prayed, saying He wants us to be in the world but not of the world (John 17:15–16). Do not be afraid. He will help you be successful in this area of your Christian walk. God bless you!

7

Be Conscious of God's Leadership

"About noon the following day as they were on their journey and approaching the city, Peter went up on the roof to pray. He became hungry and wanted something to eat, and while the meal was being prepared, he fell into a trance. He saw heaven."
—Acts 10:9–17 (NIV)

Be Conscious of God's Leadership

Introduction

The Bible is full of stories about God speaking to mankind. History tells story after story about man receiving leadership from Almighty God. Why would it be different now? But how does God make Himself known? How do we know it is really Him? Is it dreams? Is it pillars of fire and cloud as it was with Moses and the children of Israel? Is it Bill Cosby's tiny dinner bell, "ding" and "Noah?" Does an angel come down from heaven as with the virgin Mary? How can God lead me? How can God lead you?

The Bible, God's Word, contains the most important leadership for all Christians. Therein is the plan of salvation for mankind. Therein is the history of God reaching down to man. Therein are the prophecies already fulfilled and the ones about the future. Therein are the guidelines for daily living. The Bible is God's final authority in this world. God will never lead you in a way that violates or is contrary to His written Word, the Bible! Nothing supersedes the authority of the Bible. Nothing!

But, taking all that into account, God still has plans for your life that may or may not be written down in the Bible. These can be very specific, applying to just you or can be very general and apply to us all. The specific kind can be hard to know. These plans are just not going to materialize in your life automatically. You will have to seek God for leadership. The devil will try to confuse you and put you off target. See yourself comparable to an infant baby just home from the hospital if you have just become a Christian. God is not expecting much from you at this point: eating, sleeping, and growing. Do those spiritual things! This chapter seeks to explain some possibilities and offer some guidelines in finding God's general and specific will.

God's Plan for Your Life

Doesn't it seem strange the Creator God of the entire universe has plans for you and me? With billions and billions of people in the world, that He might even have a specific something for you to accomplish? He does have some kind of plan for you! For instance, what would God's plan be for you, say, tomorrow? There is one. It is a very general plan we would draw from His written Word, but a plan nonetheless. Some of God's plan for each of us, then, is general and applies to all Christians. Tomorrow's plan for someone who has been with God for some time and is already following a specific plan, would include the general plan and would have specifics applying to their life only. Don't get overwhelmed here! It's not that difficult. Tomorrow's plan for me, for instance, includes the general plan I'm about to share with you and specifics like writing this book. The "writing this book" part would not be in your plan for tomorrow, and if God has a specific plan for you tomorrow, it would not be in my plan for tomorrow. Catch all that? Okay then, what is tomorrow's plan? General guidelines of God's Word applying to all Christians can be viewed as tomorrow's plan: the ten commandments (Exodus

20); challenges to draw close to God (James 5:8b); challenges to love Him with all our heart, soul, and strength (Deuteronomy 6:4); or say, to be obedient to His Word (John 14:15–23). Most Christians do not have "tomorrow's plan" written down in their calendars. It's something we learn and constantly try to practice. But important just the same! If we never learn to obey the general guidelines of tomorrow's plan, God will never trust us with more specific plans (Luke 16;10–11)! Each of us are challenged to strive to live as closely to the general plan as possible and to listen for something more.

In the Old Testament, we read the story of Samuel, a small boy taken to live with the priest and learn the ways of the priesthood. He went to the priest because of a promise his mother made to God while praying for God's help to have a child. The general will for Samuel's life became the process of learning the ways of the priesthood. One night, Samuel heard someone calling him as he slept. He went to the high priest, his teacher, and said, "Here I am." Eli, the priest, said he had not called Samuel and sent him back to bed. This happened three times. On the third time, Eli realized God was possibly speaking to Samuel and instructed Samuel to say when he heard the voice again, "Speak, Lord, for your servant hears." When Samuel went back to bed, God did speak, and Samuel received a specific message to give to Eli the priest about the sinfulness of the priest's household (1 Samuel 1, NKJV). Delivering this message became the specific will of God for Samuel to accomplish. God may want to get that specific with you.

As we live the Christian life, doing the general will of God day by day, we should listen for God's voice. You may not know it's God speaking when it happens the first time either, like Samuel. But sooner or later, God will speak to reveal some short-term plan. "New convert, speak to that person about church," or "New Christian, attend this or that conference," or "New Christian, I'd like you to change that attitude." Who knows what God might say! But He has and does reveal short-term plans for us regularly. Also, God has some short-term prearranged plans for you in a more general sense. I can tell you now God wants you to study and learn and grow! "Study to show yourself approved" (2 Timothy 2:15, AKJV). It is part of the plan for you! He wants you to seek after Him with real intensity as the major priority in your life. "Seek first the kingdom of God" (Matthew 6:33, ESV). He wants you to share your faith as opportunity presents itself. "Follow Me and I will make you fishers of men" (Matthew 4:19/ Matthew 16:24, KJV). He wants you to share with your lifestyle every day and with your voice when He opens the door. "Let your light so shine before men" (Matthew 5:16, KJV). These are plans already revealed in His Word, which God expects from each of us, usually not "tomorrow" for new Christians, but, sooner or later, on a short-term basis.

You might ask, "How can I ever know God is speaking to me?" That would be a very valid question, but not one so difficult it has no answer. Later in this chapter, I will give you a "formula" of sorts for finding God's will. Here, however, let me give you some general guidelines about how God speaks and leads. First of all, let me remind you of the comments in the opening paragraph of this chapter: the Bible is God's final authority in this world, and the devil will try to confuse you.

Since the Bible is God's final authority in this world and since in it God says things like, "Thou shall not commit murder," and "Thou shall not commit adultery," never will God, speaking in your mind or in a dream or vision or in any way, tell you to do these things! *He never violates His written word!* So strange cult leaders who poison and kill people are *not* doing God's will regardless of what they say! Don't blame that stuff on God! And people who call themselves Christians, ministers, or anyone who is committing adultery and saying, "God knows what I'm doing, and it is okay," is lying to you and to themselves. God will never lead you to do something in violation of His written

Word. His Word, the Bible, is the final authority here. There are no exceptions to this rule!

Almost as constant, the devil will try to confuse or mislead you every time he can (1 Peter 5:8). However, stop with me a moment, and let's look realistically at the very casual way we speak to the devil. The devil himself is *not* omnipresent (everywhere at once) like God is. He is a being who can only be in one place at a time. He does have demon helpers working with him to cause confusion, evil, and deception in our lives whenever they can (Matthew 25:41; Revelation 12:7–9). But for us to fear the power of the devil himself, as always specifically directed at us, would not be correct. And we need not fear the devil and his demons if we follow after Christ anyway (Revelation 1:17–18). But in this area of being led by God or confused by the devil, we must be careful. The devil does have counterfeit methods that closely resemble the leadership of God. We must stay close to God in order to tell the difference. Did you, even as a non-Christian, recognize the voice of God as He spoke to you when you became a Christian? Sure you did; you became a Christian. God is able to make Himself known. We know, at least, in the one example, you did recognize His voice. Now let's take this a step further and say I could put my mother, Mother Hubbard, and your mother in a room together. You and I would stand in the next room, not being able to see into the room with the mothers. Each of the mothers would say hello to you. Would you recognize your mother's voice? Unless your background is of a very unusual nature (and some are), you would, of course. Could you tell the difference between my mother and Mother Hubbard? Unless your background is even more unusual, you would not. Why did you recognize your mother? Because, of course, you are very familiar with that voice. You can recognize God's for the very same reason! The closer you are to Him, the more you converse with Him, the more you seek His direction and allow Him to speak with you, the less likely you are to be confused by a counterfeit. *Put yourself in and keep yourself in a position of closeness to God!* You can minimize the confusion from the devil by staying close to God and talking to Him regularly.

God does also have some sort of long-term plan for your life. As with the other kinds of leadership, this might be a general will, applicable to all Christians, or can get very specific. In a general sense, God wants you to live for Him and go to heaven for eternity (John 3:16–17/John 14:1–3). He wants you to have spiritual impact on those around you (2 Corinthians 3:1–3). He wants you to rear your children to follow Him (Deuteronomy 6:6–9/Proverbs 22:6). He wants you to follow all the written commands of His written Word (John 14:15–23). You get the idea. This general plan is for all Christians, including you, for all your life! But also, God can get very specific about long-term plans. Many times, we in the Christian community refer to this specific long-term plan as a "calling." For example, (these time frames do not fit every leadership of God; they are meant for *explanation purposes only*) God does call people into long-term temporary positions (one-, two-, five-year terms) and also into long-term medium-ranged positions (five- to ten-year terms) and into lifetime positions (Exodus 31:1–11/Acts 16:6–10/Hebrews 5:1–10). Some people sense God's leadership for a few short years to foreign missionary work, and others, to ministry for a lifetime. Some people are led into medicine; some, into business; and others, into law. Some people never sense a specific calling from God. The possibilities are as limitless as the mind of God. As you grow as a Christian, if you will be conscious and obedient to the general will of God, and if you will keep your mind and will open to God, you may hear God's voice concerning a more specific calling. Probably since you are reading this book, you are a relatively new Christian. Be patient. Be faithful. Be listening!

One thing to keep in mind here, whether you ever receive a calling or not, is that God does still want you to be faithful to use the gifts He has given to you. This is a topic for another chapter, but one does not have to have a calling in order to be busy and useful for God using the talents and gifts God has blessed them with.

The Dependency Paradox

You may have heard the statement, "The voice of God will never lead you where the power of God cannot keep you." This is simply saying God has the power to guard our souls, keep us safe, or help us through any situation into which He might have lead us. But not only *can* God keep us but He *wants* to keep us! God wants you to depend upon Him!

We are made, if you recall the Genesis account of creation, in God's image and likeness (Genesis 1:26, 27, Genesis 5:3, Genesis 9:6). Our cognitive abilities are superior to all other such creations of God's. Our strength and ability to reason out situations makes us different and all but self-sufficient. And mankind has the tendency to act just that way—self sufficient—even toward God. The rationale goes something like this. We don't mean to cut God out, necessarily. We just don't depend upon others when we can do it ourselves. God gave to us the personality, the gifts and talents, and the abilities we have. Shouldn't we use them? And the answer, of course, is yes! *But* God still wants us to depend upon Him. There is the paradox: God created us basically self-sufficient, and yet He wants us to depend upon Him! This is not a very easy part, but it is necessary part of the Christian walk.

How This Works Against Us

When we are going through the process of life and everything is running fairly smooth, we have that natural tendency to depend upon ourselves. As such, we drift away from God because we are not going to Him with everyday problems and pains. Then comes the crisis. One day, your five-year-old falls down the stairs to the basement, injuring his head, and the doctors are saying he might not pull through. What good is medical insurance then? What good are retirement benefits then? What good is the premium job then? You are not sufficient enough then to help your son! Who can (2 Corinthians 12:9)? Only God. But what if you no longer have a relationship with Him? You have drifted away! The dependency paradox has worked against you.

Or your husband or wife comes home from "golf" or "shopping" late one afternoon and says, "I think I want a divorce." Your jaw drops to the floor. Your stomach suddenly has a panic-stricken sickening feeling. You realize the old adage was true again, and you are the last to know! Your minds reel as you think about the house, the children, and where you'll get enough income. And who is sufficient enough to help you now? You have drifted away from God and feel terribly alone (Matthew 11:28).

Maybe it's just a decision. You go to work one day, and your boss offers you a promotion. It's a great step up, but it's in Hong Kong. What do you decide? How will a move away from your husband or wife's family affect your marriage? How will change in schools and culture affect your kids? You won't have the supportive friends over there. How will you talk with your neighbors? Will this work? Can you do that job under these circumstances? Who can know (James 1:5)? This is how the dependency paradox works against us. *You must somehow realize on your best day, your very best day ever, you will still desperately need God!* (Read again!) He is the ingredient in our lives that helps us to survive and to bloom. Don't ever let the success of life convince you, even subconsciously, you are self-sufficient. Be very careful not to fall into that trap unaware! It is a natural process you will have to combat against! (Israel, throughout the Old Testament, did well as God blessed them then, in a generation or two, forgot who God was and fell away from His ways and received His judgment.) God can care for you, and He wants to care for you (2

Timothy 1:12)! This is crucial! (New convert, reread this section!) Depend upon God!

Finding God's Will

For one to seek, find, and know God's will is beyond the realm of understanding for most non-Christian people. Many Christian people struggle with this. You will not win a lot of friends and influence a lot of the world by telling them you can talk with, understand, and get answers from God. In the early Bill Cosby story of "Noah," Noah is complaining to God about several things, ("What is rain?" and "Have you looked in the bottom of that ark?" and "Who's gonna clean up that mess?") including trying to introduce God to one of his friends. "God, Larry. Larry, God," and nothing from God. Noah was embarrassed! And sometimes, now, it may seem like that when you're trying to show someone what God has said to you. For a person who does not know God and for some who do, this is something they cannot fathom. They do not have the power of the Holy Spirit to help their understanding, and so this type of conversation seems impossible. Regardless all that, if the Creator God of the universe wishes to converse with the creation, do we really think He cannot find a way? And if He says things like, "Come to Me" (Matthew 11:28, KJV) and "If any man lack wisdom, let him ask of God" (James 1:5, KJV) and "Therefore do not be like them. For the Father knows the things you have need of before you ask Him. In this same manner, therefore, pray: Our Father in heaven" (Matthew 6:8–9, NKJV), then obviously, He has provided a way for us to communicate with Him. So if we can communicate with Him and He with us and He has a plan for us as we have already discussed, then seeking and finding God's will for situations in our lives makes perfect sense. As a matter of fact, it does not make sense to live in a manner where one does not seek the wisdom and leadership of the omniscient (all-knowing) Creator God!

Seeking and finding God's will in any given situation is, without doubt, the secret to life! It's like searching and finding the mythical fountain of youth. It's like finding a formula that would cure aids or cancer. The entire world would love to find these things, if they exist, and would focus huge media attention on you if you found them. Most of the people of the world today long for power of one kind or another: if we could only make that one deal, if we could only buy the right stock at the right time, if we could just one time know the right lottery numbers, if we could marry the prince or princess. So if they could use God in their own way, many would love to plug in to the all-knowing, all-powerful, everywhere-present God of the Universe. But since God cannot be used in such ways (James 4:3) or because they do not really believe, the world seeks to do its own thing and have its own way. But the all-knowing, all-powerful, everywhere-present Power Source is still there and willing to help you if you will truly serve Him (John 9:31). There is no place of greater happiness than when we plug in to and truly serve Him. When we really sell out to God, when we give ourselves completely to Him, is when we finally find happiness and fulfillment (Philippians 1:21). That's a part of the paradox. But how do we plug in to the Power Source and find the center of God's will? There is a way!

Formula for Knowing God's Will

For ease of understanding, let me describe this in the way I do it. You can use the same principles and do it in your own way, but to make it understandable to everyone, I will lay this out in the manner I can describe it best—the way I do it!

When I am seeking an answer or seeking leadership from God, the first thing I consider is God's interest in me. He is the One who sent the Son. He is the One who offers the Written Word. He is the One reaching down to me. It helps me to remember God is like a good parent interested in the smallest and largest of my questions or problems. He is waiting for me and for you to ask (Matthew 6:8 and 7:7). Don't hesitate to take your situation to God; He is thrilled!

Secondly, I remember my limitations in communicating and understanding Almighty God. He can read my thoughts. He understands the intent of my heart. He knows my future. I have no such advantages in trying to understand Him. I seek to receive answers from God in the simplest format possible. I ask questions most of the time that require yes/no answers if at all possible. I only seek to find one answer at a time to avoid my confusion. This process brings a humorous story I have heard to mind: A man's property was flooding from a time of spring rains. When the water got to the first floor of his house, he began to move all his belongings upstairs. A neighbor in a rowboat came by and offered to take him to higher ground. He refused, saying, "God will take care of me." Later, as the water reached the second story of his house, a stranger came by in a motorboat and tried to convince him to leave. He again refused and said, "God will take care of me." The water continued to rise, and he was soon out on his roof looking a sea of water all around. A coast guard helicopter spotted him and came to lift him to safety, but he waved them off, shouting something about God taking care of him. The story picks up in heaven after the man drowns and he is mad at God and questioning why God let him drown! God says, "I sent you a rowboat, a motorboat, and a helicopter. What did you want?" *The man was seeking his answer but had never understood God was speaking to him!* Because of our limited, finite minds vs. God's infinite knowledge and wisdom, even taking into account the humanity of Christ and the measureless benevolence of God, a kind of lopsided communication must occur. We must be careful to structure a question so from our point of reference, we understand God's answer.

Then I remember the devil is out there trying to confuse me as much as possible. He is trying to put me off track, and I resolve to do this carefully and prayerfully! Then I set up the structure as a backdrop for me to understand God's voice or leadership.

Prayer is supposed to be a two-way conversation with God, so how do you listen?" I'm always amazed at the number of people who say to me at this point they "just go with how they feel." It seems to me if it's important enough to ask God about in the first place, then one should make sure the response from God is clearly understood. Numbers of people, even ministers, have said to me here, "I should never have made that move," or "I wish I could make that decision again." God does not promise to eliminate human mistakes. What we can do, however, is seek and know God's leadership for our lives in a way that allows us to look back without major regrets.

I try to keep a prayer journal every day (I'm not successful every day). I use it to keep a record of the kinds of things I'm going through and how God is leading me. I use this journal as a record-keeping place for important leadership from God. Let's say I'm faced with a decision about changing ministry locations, with a decent-sized financial decision, or a decision about a problem in my church. I take it to God in prayer. Then expecting God to answer, I carefully construct the question to God. "God, are you leading me to leave the place of ministry where I am?" or "God, do I approach this problem person in my church now?" One step at a time. I know I am slow, and I want to be sure. Yes or no is fine with me; as a matter of fact, I prefer it! I'm ready now, and I write that carefully constructed question into my journal addressed to God.

Now the following system or formula I follow is not my own. I probably use some of my own terms and my own structure, but I have heard these points preached and taught most of my life. They find their roots in God's Word and in years of experience. These have been proven successful over and over again. I challenge you not to change the points themselves. Put them in your own words or set up if you like, but follow the proven guideline.

In my journal, under the carefully constructed question, I list the four points of the formula with room to make notes over the following days or weeks. I consistently, then, take the question to God in prayer and dutifully go back to the place in the journal where the question is written down and note the leadership I receive from the Lord in its proper place within the structure of the formula. Within a day or two, a week or two, or maybe it takes a month, the answer takes form and becomes very clear. Is it fool-proof? No! But it does successfully eliminate most of the opportunities for the devil to confuse, for our own feelings to interfere, or for us to jump into a major mistake, and it gives God opportunity to give leadership. It works!

By the way, as I have carefully approached this formula, trying to include all I do, I am reminded many times the devil's trick here is to get us to rush to make a mistake. If you feel rushed in making a decision, it's almost always the devil trying to put you off track. God is not the "author of confusion" (1 Corinthians 14:33, KJV) and, as such, will give you plenty of time to come to a decision. God rarely rushes anyone. Take your time.

Again then, first I write the carefully composed question. Then under the question, I write:

1. Scripture:
2. Holy Spirit in my conscience:
3. Open/Closed door:
4. Christian friends/confidantes:

These are the four points of the formula. They are listed one to four, in order of importance. Scripture is always most important. But all the points are used together as a formula. As I pray and approach God over the next days, I constantly say, "And, God, what about my question?" and I listen. I share my question with some very close friends and some I have spiritual confidence in and ask them to pray. I ask them to give me feedback concerning any impression or leadership they receive from God. I look for doors of opportunity to open up or close down in relation to this question. As I do my devotional reading, I am careful to observe any scriptures that stand out to me speaking to my question. I don't close my eyes, open the Bible, and point. I don't use my familiarity with scripture to look for specific answers. If any thing, I avoid familiar scriptures. I let God make a scripture stand out to me during my regular, daily reading. Any tidbit of information from any of the four sources, I list in its proper place in the outline of the formula. Gradually, they all form a picture of God's will. At some point then, I realize I am looking at a written picture of God's leadership! That's a great feeling.

You ready for this? I don't always accept this first answer from God. Whoa, you say! And God does not strike you down? God is never offended if we are sincerely seeking His will! If I still have any reservations about this question of leadership, then I may say to God with real humbleness of heart, "Lord, please let's do this all again. New scriptures, new speaking to my conscience, new doors of opportunity, and new friends involved." God is not offended! God does not rush! He knew in advance what I would ask. In the book of Judges in the Old Testament, a story is told of Gideon being led by God to free His people from the Midianite oppression. I'm going to ask you to stop soon and read the story in chapters 6 and 7 of Judges; but not just yet.

As you read, you will see that Gideon took lots of time in being assured of God's will. Gideon went back to God more than once, asking the same question. God was not offended. God was pleased with Gideon from the beginning and so picked him for the job, and not only answered his questions, but in the end, offered another reassurance of God's leadership and promise of success (Judges 7:9–14). God will work with you in an effort for you to be sure of His leadership and will! He will not rush. He will not push. He will give you room and time if you are sincerely seeking and wanting to know His leadership. Stop now and read.

Pretty neat, huh? You can converse with and receive leadership from the all-knowing, all-powerful, everywhere-present God of the Universe. New Christian, God wants to be close to you. He is waiting for you to show your interest in being close to Him. Make your mind up to live a life of being directed by God. Make the decision to give your life to God, not just your heart. There is a difference. (You will read more of that in book 2.)

God Will Not Forsake You

This "knowing God's will" business is a little scary, isn't it? Sometimes, I believe, we think if we do not get it all quite right, God goes off and leaves us. We have been taught in times past that God is waiting with a bolt of lighting and, if we get out of line a little, is anxious to zap us. In fact, nothing could be further from the truth! God is loving, patient, and never leaves us! Read the story of David, the king, when he got completely off track, took another man's wife, and had him killed in battle (2 Samuel 11 and 12:25). God disciplined David, and the son of the union died. God did not, however, forsake David. God was patient and merciful, and in fact, Jesus's line of heritage comes straight through Solomon, the next son of that union. God did not move away from David at all. In the New Testament (John 8:1–11), when the Pharisees brought a woman caught in adultery to Jesus and demanded He follow the law in punishing her (Jewish Old Testament law demanded stoning to death for adultery), He said to them, "He who is without sin among you, let him throw a stone first" (John 8:7, KJV). When they finally all walked away because of their own sin, Jesus said to this woman, "Neither do I condemn you, go and sin no more" (John 8:11, KJV). God's position is consistent. He is merciful, kind, loving, patient, and never leaves us. You cannot fool God! If you are not sincere in asking forgiveness or if you just say, "I can do what I want. God will forgive me," He may not. (Remember the "slap in the face" story?) But all in all, God gives us lots of time to get it right. He is not waiting to strike you with lighting but rather waiting to help you every way you will let Him. If you get away from God, you will have to purposefully walk away.

Listen and Obey

You are growing now, new Christian, and more and more opportunities will exist for you to obey God. Make a lifestyle of listening and obeying God. Spend time alone with God, and give Him time to talk to you. You can know His will in a general sense by reading His Word. You can know His will in a specific sense by asking, seeking, knocking, and listening (Matthew 7:7). If you wish your life to be happy and complete in the Lord, if you wish to lead your family in the way of the Lord, and if you wish to make heaven your home some day, then I challenge you to make a life of listening and following after the will of God. God bless you in your efforts. I'm praying for you!

8

Your Pastor/Discipler

"Now we ask you, brothers, to respect those who work hard
among you, who are over you in the Lord and
who admonish you. Hold them in the
highest regard in love because of their work."
—1 Thessalonians 5:12–13 (NIV)

Your Pastor/Discipler

Roles of the Pastor/Discipler

I remember when the first of my four daughters was born. I was way young—only twenty. It was during the Vietnam War. I had received a draft number of forty-nine, subsequently joined the army, and now I was training at Fort Carson, Colorado. It happened about three thirty in the afternoon without difficulty or unusual incident. We were out there from our home state of Ohio all alone. No family members came out to join us at this critical time. Then suddenly, I had the major responsibility of caring for a child. It was now the responsibility of mother and father to feed, care for, teach, protect, mold, and inspire new infant life. What an awesome trust! What an overwhelming position! Could we do this? Could we do this right? Could we do this well? This is the same position, the same trust, the same fears your pastor has before God about you!

In the writings of the Apostle Paul in the New Testament, he says he tries to become "all things to all people" that he might win some to Christ (1 Corinthians 9:19–23, KJV). This is the same principle; your pastor, if you have one, is likely trying to follow in some pattern of evangelism and discipleship. Your pastor is a person reaching out to you in understanding and attempted help; a person trying to understand where you are coming from so he/she can be for you whatever you need like Paul. Your pastor is, within reasonable limits, probably willing to be available to you at almost any time. Of course, he/she has times assigned to others, and/or you may be assigned to another discipler altogether. This is very acceptable. But as a new Christian, help with questions and leadership is probably available to you almost any time. If this is not true and you are struggling, you need to ask more questions and/or look for a solid church that is willing to train you.

I don't want to be too critical here, but allow me for the sake of those in unwholesome situations to make a couple of generalized comments. This area of winning and disciplining others for Christ is not some new idea. God's Word is very specific about this (Matthew 28:19–20). Churches and pastors have specific responsibilities before God. So for those of you reading this who find yourselves in a less-than-ideal setting, not where you are just looking for an excuse, but where discipleship is not happening for you, let me make a couple of suggestions. Go ask your pastor for help. Go ask some older Christian for some help. They may not be aware of your need. If that does not or has not worked, listen up. You don't know why someone has reacted to you in a way that has not met your need. God doesn't give you the right to judge. Simply look for a place or a godly person who will meet your need. If you are in such a situation, don't let it turn you away from God. Regardless of how you have been treated, you are still ultimately responsible for your own spiritual situation. Would you never go to another doctor or gas station if you had bad experiences there? Of course not! Don't overreact if you have had a bad experience at a church. That is not an excuse that will ever hold up with God. Just because the Klu Klux Klan quotes scripture and uses the cross doesn't make them Christian. And just because you have not had your need met at a particular place does not mean they are not Christian or that you have found the right spot. Give God and yourself another chance and go where you can get help. Your eternal soul hangs in the balance. Don't let the devil trick you out of your salvation because of an unhealthy situation.

I realize everyone reading this will not have a pastor of their own. You need one! Or some of you reading this will have a pastor who seems not to genuinely care. Please don't use me or this book as an excuse to leave a good church. But at the same time, a pastor and church willing to invest in your new spiritual life is critical. Find a church offering something for new Christians—not talking here about membership, but new converts or new Christians. Let that be your guide. If a church has a class or study for new Christians or is willing to create one, then there likely is a place you can go for the spiritual help you need. Go there. If someone led you to Jesus Christ, ask him or her about a church. Don't just go to any church because it is a church, because it is convenient, or because you have had some association with them before. Go to a place and to a pastor who will nurture you! The nurturing relationship is what this chapter and book is about.

Allow me to be graphic. Let's say mother and father brought that first baby girl home, went straight to the nursery, and laid her down in the cradle. "Welcome home, baby girl," they said, and left the room, closing the door after them. One week later, they come back to the nursery and open the door to what? Huh? That's right, a dead baby! Babies require constant care and help! They cannot feed themselves! They cannot dress themselves! They cannot clean or groom themselves! They are at the mercy of those who are supposed to take care of them. You are that spiritual baby!

As I write this, we are nursing baby puppies. Their mother, our nine-year-old English springer spaniel who refused earlier in life to breed, surprised us with a man about town and then died two weeks after giving birth. My oldest daughter at home has become the puppies' mother. She feeds them, cleans them, cuddles them, and, in the beginning of this process, even helped them learn to urinate by rubbing their bellies with a warm cotton ball. Yuck! She is an excellent puppy mother, getting up in the night to feed and love them. This is not always a great gig! If it is not done and done well, the puppies will die. This is a perfect example for us! Christian discipleship is not always easy and clean! But as an infant Christian, you need the help of mature Christians in showing you the way to survive and thrive spiritually. God is your power and strength, but other Christians are a great help in guiding you toward the right things of God. That fellowship-relationship is a critical one!

Nursery Attendant

Again, unless you have a lot of spiritual background from a younger time in life, you are an infant Christian. As such, allow the following comparison.

When you take your children for others to care for, be it Grandma and Grandpa, a day-care center, a nursery at church, a local teenager, or a childcare center at the mall, it is a relationship similar to your relationship with those Christians charged with your care. You expect, for instance, for those caring for your children to maintain a controlled environment. You expect them to protect your children within this environment. You do not want your children playing in the street. You do not want your children drinking cleaning solvents. You do not want your children watching explicit material on TV. You want the sitters to maintain a safe environment. And you do not want the sitters cooking your children in the microwave. Your disciplers are charged with similar responsibilities. They cannot hold your hand every moment, and you are an adult responsible for your own salvation (Philippians 2:12), but your disciplers want to protect and provide for you as much as they can.

They will want to comment about your everyday environment. They will not want you to play in the spiritual street where the devil can hit you with a truck (1 Peter 5:8). They will not want you to play under the spiritual sink where you can drink deadly spiritual chemicals. They will not want you to read or watch material that will confuse you or pull you away from God. You are a spiritual infant, and they are your spiritual sitters. Allow your pastor or discipler the necessary input to help you. Listen to what they say!

When you take your children to the child care center to spend the day, you also expect them to feed them. And, of course, you are happy if they feed them junk food and sugars just before you get them back at bedtime, right? Not!

Your spiritual disciplers will want to have input about your spiritual food. They will want you to read material like this and to study the Bible. As you have questions, they may want you to read other books. They will encourage you to be in church and to attend special new Christian classes. They will likely also push you toward fellowship times like group dinners, special church activities, church-related sports involvements, etc. All these varied interests in you are attempts by your pastor/discipler to help you attach and grow spiritually. They are attempts to help you get to heaven.

Your pastor/discipler should be your key "answer guy." He or she is the one you should get explanations from as you have questions. Your pastor/discipler can explain your new world. The Bible teaches us as we become Christians we become new creations in Christ (2 Corinthians 5:17–18). This new life will take some adjustments and changes. You should have lots of questions. Let's say you had recently joined the army. Would you automatically know how to march, where to eat, when to get up and go to bed, how to dismantle your weapon, where to find medical help, and so on? You would have to listen to endless briefings (take my word for it!) and/or ask lots of questions. The army said to me, "There are no stupid questions! Stupid is getting hurt or in trouble for not asking a question." The same should be practiced here. Do the same here in God's army. And expect your pastor/discipler to answer the majority of those questions. Again, if you had joined the US Army, you would not expect your neighbor or the taxi driver to answer questions about military protocol, about weapons and the mess hall! Ask your pastor and don't give the devil the opportunity to confuse you with an answer that is incorrect or misleading from someone else.

All these roles are the roles of the nursery attendant caring for the infant Christian. I challenge you not to fight the "baby Christian" name tag and to listen to the advice of your pastor/discipler. You are in the spiritual nursery, and you will need their help to survive and thrive as a Christian.

Counselor

Another role your pastor and/or designated person in your church should fill for you is that of Counselor.

Some answers are just not cut and dry. Many topics and questions just need discussed with someone who can give you a spiritual viewpoint. This person is probably not a professional counselor but does not need to be. They are someone with insight and experience with God and do have specific interest in your spiritual well-being. If you are with some genuine Christian, and we will discuss that later, you should have no great fears about being taken advantage of as they selflessly represent Christ and not their own interest.

Many new Christians, in steering through the changes of the new lifestyle, have questions about everything. They have had ideas from times past about how to live or not to live the Christian life, and now they need to clarify those many things. In the effort to be sincere with God, and by not having a spiritual background, one can be easily confused or misled.

You have questions about regular life issues that do not seem "exactly spiritual." You may begin to question your style of child rearing or discipline. You may begin to question your style of budgeting or spending habits. You may have questions about your marriage or other relationships. These are issues with which Christian disciplers can assist you. They do not have to be just "spiritual issues." On the other hand, they might be.

Just recently, one such new Christian in my church had a question fitting into this category. One night as we talked about Christian things, after a midweek service as I recall, he asked this question, "Now just how do I pray? Do I always have to fold my hands and bow my head?" Now to some of you, that may seem a silly question, knowing God will hear us pray from any position or place. But to others of you who have had only a Sunday school background, or no background at all with spiritual things, his question may be seen as perfectly legitimate. And it was! No question should go unasked! Scripture says, "How shall they hear without a preacher?" (Romans 10:14, KJV). It turned out this new Christian was trying to drive to work in the mornings while folding his hands and bowing his head to pray at the same time. It pays to ask! Let your pastor be a counselor about as many things as he/she feels comfortable about which to answer. He/she wants what's best for you before God!

Teacher

This is an overlapping position with the counselor job. Your discipler should be a teacher to you in many areas of your life. He or she may actually teach your new-Christians class or your Bible study during the week. He or she, if also your pastor, will certainly teach at times while preaching. Also, the "teacher" will teach at almost any time you spend with them. I personally have spent time teaching new Christians almost everywhere you might care to mention: in the car, in the kitchen, in the church, in their homes, at the ball game, while on vacation, while working on a car, at meetings, while playing ball or golf, after church, while mowing the lawn, standing in the street, over dinner or lunch, in letters, on the phone local and long distance (before cell phones), and on and on. A teacher will teach any time he is given a chance. A new Christian can learn at almost any time they spend with their discipler! What a combination! Look for these opportunities!

Also, watch their life! They should exemplify or demonstrate the kind of life they are teaching to you! You must be careful here because if your discipler falls or fails, so might you! This is always a risk! I have read of situations where the leader of a stunt flying team flew into the ground and then so did his team, following Him! This is a risk you need to monitor for your own spiritual well-being. Most of the time, however, you can watch your discipler's life for its teaching value. Most of the time, they are people who are trustworthy and dedicated to God.

Christ, the Discipler

Our example is Christ, yours and mine. As our discipler, He has set the example for us. Jesus served for about three and a half years as a teacher and as a leader to the disciples. For this period of time, He literally lived with them. He ate with them, slept with them, traveled with them. They were there when He performed miracles, when He raised the dead, when He preached the Sermon on the Mount. They saw Him walk on the water, saw Peter walk on the water with Him, watched Him be arrested, be found guilty, and put to death! He was always with them. They saw and experienced it all. They learned by His example and by His mentoring. He was their role model. Your discipler can fulfill a similar role for you.

You probably cannot spend that much time with your pastor/discipler. But the point must be well taken: you can learn much from spending time with your discipler. Plato once said, "You can learn more about a person in one hour of play than in a year of work." Apply this principle to your situation of learning, and you understand you can make good use of even casual time spent with your disicpler. Classroom time is great and not to be replaced, but time spent helping your discipler do whatever he/she is doing is time well spent also. Visit people in the hospital with them. Travel to services or seminars with them. Attending casual cookouts and playing games are all valuable learning tools.

Keep in mind, however, the pastor/discipler is probably married and has a family. Be observant of the family's time. Don't invade when they are doing family things. In your pastor's system of priorities, his or her family should come before church and ministry, before you! Be sure you are not changing those priorities!

Okay, those were some of the roles of your pastor/discipler as pertaining to you. What roles should you be fulfilling?

Your Roles

At this point of your Christian walk, you are a student, a sponge, a follower. Not unlike starting a new job, you are in that "probationary process" where you stick like glue to someone who knows what they are doing. And not unlike some of those situations, you can get hurt wandering away on your own.

Your primary role is that of a student. You should be trying to learn all you can about Christ and being a Christian. Just like in school, you need to listen when being taught. You need to watch what's going on around you. You need to question everything you don't understand. You need to read God's Word. There is no substitute for spending time in the Bible! That's where Christ is explained to us. That's where Christ most often speaks to us! That's where we can study His life. Time spent studying the Bible is time spent that cannot be replaced with any other thing. All these things are involved in the role of a student. Be a good student! Making an *A* here pays dividends in eternity. Failing here has spiritual death written all over it.

I'm not trying to set your pastor/discipler up in a role that they cannot fulfill. But they do have a responsibility before God and one of which they are probably well aware. You become the student to this person, the mentored one in this relationship. For this, you also have responsibility before God! Allow them to give you direction, help, and support.

As sermons are preached, as Sunday school classes are taught, as Bible Studies happen, as examples are set before you, as you study the life of Christ and begin to pattern after Him, as questions are answered, as the picture slowly begins to take shape around you, be a sponge and suck it all up! Suck up, store, and retain as much of all this as you possibly can! The more input you can accumulate and process and strain through God's Word, (Philippians 2:12 and 2 Timothy 2:15), the better Christian you are going to be.

I will never forget, nor I doubt will anyone who was there, an incident that happened in my presence when I was a teenager. It involved my father, the pastor, and an older man from the community. Our church had been growing for some time, was planning to build, and bought the rest of the properties all the way to the corner to the west of the church. This purchase included several properties, including one small house, which, at this time, had been bought, paid for, and the older man who had lived there was moved away. It was a little place with a green roof and painted siding. I remember the eves of this place were barely high enough to stand under, and it wasn't bigger than three or four rooms in size. It was a Saturday workday, and many of the men of the church were on the property cleaning up, removing all the unwanted trash, and burning it. The fire got hot and although not out of control, started blistering the paint on the side of that small house some yards away. Well, the former occupant, the older man who had lived there, had wandered back down the street from his new house and was observing the process when he noticed the blistering paint on his old house. Although no one else cared because it was going to be torn down, he must have still had some emotional ties to the old place. The blistering paint made him angry, and he approached my father and began to yell and scream. All the guys of the church turned to see what was happening, including me, and thus the impact of this story. What kind of role model would the pastor be in this kind of difficult situation? He must have been aware of all the eyes of the church, and I wonder now if he was consciously aware of the eyes of his impressionable teenage son. The older man was a big guy. My father was well over six foot tall, and this guy was at least that tall and outweighed my father. The old guy was pointing and yelling, and suddenly he slugged my father with his right hand to the left side of Dad's face. It makes me emotional even now to tell the story. Then I just saw a strange incident that my dad passed off as "no big deal." Now, I see a type of Christ in full control, setting the right example. My father never moved. He simply stood there and continued to talk to the old fellow. The old guy hit him again! Not one movement, not one escalated word of contempt. Not even an attempt to defend himself. Nothing! Not so for others. A big farmer, the song leader of our church, Harold Walters, put his arms around this guy from behind, picked him up off the ground, and walked away. It was over as fast as it had started, but the godly example would last a lifetime in the minds of those being discipled.

Suck up the example of your pastor/discipler. Not that they cannot make mistakes, but for the most part, these are godly examples of how Christ wants you to live.

As the follower, you are dependant upon the discipler. You can easily die without someone to guide you. Remember the example of the baby coming from the hospital and being left alone? Don't let the devil trick you into being separated from your discipler. He will try! You will not like something they will say, do, teach, attitude displayed, or something! Don't let the devil do that to you! Again, your discipler is not perfect, but they are trying to teach you the things of God. You need to learn! I'm reminded here of a new Christian at this last pastorate of mine who made this very mistake. Even with this warning of mine in advance, he became disenchanted with me and pulled away from me and from God. This is nothing but a trick of the devil. To this very day, as far as I know, he is going to hell and would truthfully say to you and to me that he is fully aware of his position. I'm sure I have some accountability before God for something (he would never admit a reason), but he is fully accountable for his soul. Sad! Sad! Sad!

On the other hand, you can die spiritually if you follow your discipler and he or she is incorrect! How's that for a difficult spot? Any time you put yourself into one of these dependent relationships, you become somewhat vulnerable. It can be a tricky situation for a new Christian. You need to keep your common sense about you! All the commands for you are also applicable to your discipler. If you are closely watching their life and what you see is sin, then back up and make sure of what you saw. Your discipler's reputation is on the line. Be careful. If you become sure, go to an older Christian, a board member, a deacon, or elder and ask for help. But if what you see is sin, don't follow the example! Don't lose focus on Christ and His Word! Again, everything taught to you should agree with God's Word!

We cannot forget the lessons of the 1980s when key TV evangelicals strayed off course and no doubt caused many followers to question, doubt, and lose out with God. It's not that these were bad people or never Christians at all. They were simply humans who succumbed to temptation and followed the wrong path. They were tricked by the devil! This, in turn, put them off course with God and subsequently out of the ministry. In the mean while, many people suffered with them. That won't happen too often, but be mindful of the leadership of the Holy Spirit and remember you are really following Christ.

Watch Christ

Your overall goal here is to be Christlike. Carefully learn the ways of the Master. Study His life and project Him through your everyday life. Know His attitudes. Learn His motivations. Study His reactions. Glean His humility and His obedience. Desire to be like Christ. The Apostle Paul again challenges us to take on the fruit of the Spirit: "love, joy, peace, patience, temperance, goodness, meekness," against which, he says, "there is no law" (paraphrased from Galatians 5:22–23). These are the characteristics of the Spirit of God, and we should strive to incorporate them into the core of out lives. Paul is saying everyone appreciates these characteristics. No one rebels against being treated with these attitudes. We don't make laws against treating people kindly. Learn how Christ acts, reacts, feels, and thinks to the extent we can know through His Word. That is how He wants you to be.

The Bible is full of stories of Christ and Christlike people. Some of these people are so like Christ we call them "types of Christ." They set the example for the people of their day of how Christ would be. They continue to set the example for us today because their lives have been recorded. These examples need to be studied. You will want to pattern your life after the Christlike traits of these people. Living a Christlike life does not just happen. It is not done accidentally. It took specific and intentional determination and effort on their part and will on your part.

In conjunction with this, we also find in scripture where God challenges us through Peter to be a "peculiar people" (1 Peter 2:9, KJV). Many people read this and think God wants us to stick out in society in odd fashion. They get confused about these "oddities" and dress strangely or do or act in ways that make them repulsive to people around them. That is not what God had in mind. He wants us to be peculiar for sure! But peculiar in ways that attract people to Him! He wants us to act like Him in those "fruit of the Spirit" (Galatians 5:22) ways. He wants us to treat people with acceptance and inclusiveness. He wants us to reflect the picture of Christ in Matthew, where we see Him standing with arms open wide, saying, "Come unto Me all who labor and are heavy laden and I will give you rest" (Galatians 5:22, KJV). He wants us to be peculiar in a way where we readily give to those in need. He wants us to be peculiar in a way where we reach out to help the poor, the handicapped, and the hurting of the world. All this is whom Jesus was when He lived in the flesh here in this world. This is who He wants us to be now. In Luke 10:25–37, we read the story of the "Good Samaritan." Here was a man who could be expected to act in a way different from what he did. The injured man was Jewish, and the traveler was Samaritan. Samaritans were half-Jewish, and the two races had become enemies. The traveler acted so "peculiarly" to how others expected him to act that we still use the term "Good Samaritan" to describe someone acting with kindness two thousand years later! No one wants to make laws against acting as a "Good Samaritan." "Peculiar" doesn't seem too bad? There's Christ idea for us! Be Christlike like this Samaritan!

In this new Christian walk, along side your discipler, let me again challenge you to follow with an eye on scripture. All humans make mistakes. The best of disciplers sometimes do or say things that are misunderstood. The worst of disciplers may be someone filling a role they are not qualified to fill. Be trusting but cautious enough not to allow yourself to lose out with God because of an imperfect human example. I don't mention this again because I think bad disciplers are a big problem in the church today. I mention this because I see and talk with many former Christians who were turned off by someone who acted impulsively or incorrectly, most never thinking of the negative impact on others. Understand you are responsible for your eternal soul! Regardless of what others do or say, how it hurts, or how much you don't understand how a Christian could be that way, it's still your soul! Why would anyone ever take the position, "I don't want anything to do with God/church if that is how Christians are," yet we have all heard that said. I have heard it way too many times! Don't allow anyone to separate you from your newfound eternal life. Don't confuse the Christian you are watching with Christ!

As you grow and become more stable, you will get to the place where you feel strong enough to stand on your own spiritually. In fact, none of us ever get to the place where we never need anyone. Don't let the devil so trick you. You can, however, get to the place where you do not need the constant oversight of the discipler. Your view of Christ is a little more direct at this point. At this time, you begin to look directly to Christ instead of looking at Christ through the eyes of your discipler. It is like a physical baby, you need to grow to the place of enough strength to stand on your own.

You control your own growth. This is much like those homeschool programs where the student progresses at their own pace. In James 4:8a (NLT), the writer says, "Draw close to God and God will draw close to you." The more you move toward God, the more He moves toward you. As you study and learn and allow God to adjust your attitudes and actions, as you humble yourself before Him and become more like Him, as you become a new creation in Christ Jesus, the more likely you are able to stand. This is not a race in the sense you need to sprint to this point of your Christian experience, but either you are growing at this stage of your walk or there is something wrong. Again, just as in the life of a physical baby, early days, weeks, months, and years are the times of the most learning and growth.

College degrees are not needed to sincerely study the Word of God. Don't be backed off by the fact it is not completely easy. Part of the job of the Holy Spirit of God is helping us understand the Word (John 16;12–14). If you approach the study of God's Word seriously, you will be rewarded and learn. You can always go back to your pastor/discipler and verify your approach to study. You can always ask if what you have learned is valid. They will always be ready to help you. And God will never fail you! He will reward and feed the sincere student. Make the effort to learn, grow, and stand on your own. It is only then God can really begin to use you.

This is an exciting time, new Christian. Press on! God has much more in store for you. Your pastor/discipler is a great resource and growth coach. Depend upon them. Depend upon God even more and grow, grow, grow!

9

Giving to God

"I am the true vine, and my Father is the gardener. He cuts off every branch in Me that bears no fruit, while every branch that does bear fruit He prunes so that it will be even more fruitful. You are already clean because of the word I have spoken to you. No branch can bear fruit by itself; it must remain in the Vine. Neither can you bear fruit unless you remain in Me. I am the Vine; you are the branches. If a man remains in Me and I in him, he will bear much fruit; apart from Me you can do nothing. If anyone does not remain in Me, he is like a branch that is thrown away and withers; such branches are picked up, thrown into the fire and burned."

—Jesus, quoted by John in John 15:1–6 (NIV)

Giving to God

Author's Challenge

Well, new Christian, some people get weeded out right here at chapter 9. I hope you are not one of them! Please don't let the devil successfully attack you here. Take a moment before you start this chapter to pray and ask God to help you resist the devil. Again, James 4:7 (NKJV) says, "Therefore submit to God. Resist the devil and he will flee from you." Do just that! Submit to God about these issues and resist the devil by quoting this scripture and pray and rebuke Satan like Jesus did (Matthew 4:1–10), and God will help you right now!

When this business of living for God begins to "cost something," many people get somewhat less committed. During Jesus's days here on earth, when He came to the point of preaching a hard gospel, some people began to leave Him (John 6:60–66). Some of these people were following just for the free meals and the excitement of the miracles, so then, for others, when the truth began to hurt a little, their "commitment" faded (John 6). Very few things in this life have much value. Eternal life with Jesus

Christ, however, is worth whatever it might cost! Don't let the devil scare you away now. As the old song says, "You've come too far to turn back now."

Again, God's Plan for the World: Your Part

Remember God is trying to reach the whole world with the good news! Remember He created mankind out of a desire to have someone choose to love Him. So God chose to love us. Think about where you would be, where any of us would be, if not for the love of God for us! He has shown His great love for each of us by sending His Son, Jesus Christ, to die on the cross for our sins. How then should we respond? A part of the measure of our love for a person is our desire to please the person we love. God is looking for followers who love Him enough to keep His commandments and help Him spread the gospel. A part of the measure of our love for Christ, then, is our willingness to give to Him. Listen to the words of the Apostle Paul as he speaks of how God's love should affect us. "For the love of Christ compels us, because we are convinced that One died for all, and therefore all died. And He died for all that those who live should no longer live for themselves, but for Him who died for them and was raised again" (2 Corinthians 5:14–15 (NIV). Paul says we have an opportunity and an obligation of service to Christ, and he backed that statement up with a life of service and his death as a martyr. If we were called upon to give up our lives and our very life for Christ, could we? Could you? Would you? Giving can be a tough thing!

So then let's explore the principles and dynamics that allow us to give to God or, as Christians, do our part. John teaches us Jesus created all, through the power of the godhead. John 1:1–3 (NIV) says, "In the beginning was the Word, (Jesus) and the Word was with God, (the Father) and the Word was God. (John 10:30,

NIV: "I and the Father are One.") He was in the beginning with God. All things were made through Him, and without Him, nothing was made that was made." So God made all. This is the first principle of giving. *Everything that is belongs to God, even you and me.* He created us and everything else. We enjoy the benefits. We breathe the air. We soak up the sunshine. We dance in the rain and dive into the ocean. We eat of the foods of the earth. We nuzzle the babies. We ogle the sights. We enjoy the love of a companion. We zoom in fast cars and planes. We are astounded at modern technology. We talk about the speed of light like we understand it. We use His earth's minerals. We work and live and buy nice places to live. We splurge and "own" diamonds and four-wheelers and sports cars. But somewhere along the way, we tend to forget "every good and perfect gift is from above and comes down from the Father of Lights" (James 1:7, NKJV). Remember, God created all. God owns all! That's true. Everything you think you have really belongs to God. All of it. You, your children, your home and cars, your pets, your paycheck, and your potty chair. It's all God's. He allows us the use of and makes us responsible for the stewardship of all these things. (And there is a test at the end of time, by the way.) If and when we really understand this fact (He owns it all), we are free to begin to give to God.

Secondly, God's Word teaches a tithing principle. This is a giving back to Him a tenth part of what He has given to us. This is a giving back of not only a tenth part but a giving back of the first tenth part of what He gives to us. Now again, remember everything we have and receive belongs to and comes from God. And again, that includes our time, our talent, and our income. He teaches, then, to honor Him and to fuel the work of the kingdom in this world, we Christians funnel that first tenth part of what he gives us back into His church (Malachi 3:10; Mark 12:13–17; Matthew 23:23–24).

It has always been this way. The Bible begins, "In the beginning..." And just fourteen chapters later, we see Abram (later

Abraham) bring tithe of his increase to the priest Melchiezedek. A rebellion happened in the area where Abram lived, and several kings went to war with others, and in the process, Abram's nephew Lot and family were taken captive. When Abram learned of the capture, he armed his 318 servants and pursued the raiding parties. With God's help, he defeated the group and reclaimed the captured people, possessions, animals, and such, as well as the spoils of the raiding armies. When Abram returned with all these possessions, he refused to keep for himself any of these people and possessions, but he did pay a tithe to God's priest of all he had technically gained (Genesis 14).

In that earliest of time, most people did not work for cash money but lived off the yield of the land in some way. Because of that, much of scripture talks about giving that tenth portion out of what people were harvesting. Later in Leviticus, where God list to His people, the Israelites, many of His laws and commandments for them, we read the following verses. "And all of the tithes of the land, whether of the seed of the land or of the fruit of the tree, is the Lord's. It is holy to the Lord…These are the commandments which the Lord commanded Moses for the children of Israel on Mt. Sinai" (Leviticus 27:30–34 (KJV). All of which these people received of the land, they paid a tithe to God because everything belongs to God. Also in Numbers, we read, "Speak thus to the Levites, and say to them: 'When you take from the people of Israel the tithes which I have given you from them as your inheritance, then you shall offer up a heave offering of it to the Lord, a tenth of the tithe'" (Numbers 18:26 (NKJV). The Levites were the priestly tribe of Israel. It was their job to maintain the place of worship for Israel, the temple of the Lord, and many other duties. This Levite tribe, meaning the priest and all their families, did not maintain big property and fields or flocks like all the other tribes. In fact, when God, through Joshua, assigned all the areas of land to the different tribes of Israel, the Levite tribe did not receive any land (Numbers 18:20).

The Levite inheritance was God and they were to be cared for by the other tribes with their tithes and offerings. (There is a difference in tithes and offerings, and I will explain later in this chapter.) But even when the Levites received the tenth part tithe from all the other people, the priest themselves had to pay a tithe unto God of their increase, or income if you will. This tithing into the temple/church was and still is God's plan of maintaining the priestly tribe (ministers) and the temple cost (churches) and funding the spread of the gospel in the world.

The next principle is about the first tenth. In Exodus 23:19a (NKJV), we read about this idea of the tenth part being the first or first-fruits of our labors. "The first of the first-fruits of your land you shall bring into the house of the Lord your God." *This taught and maintained God as a first priority in their lives.* God is not second anything! He will not accept second place in our lives. He wants us to maintain this idea of the firstfruits. When we give Him this first tenth, we keep Him always in front of us and likely keep Him first in our lives. God knew the weaknesses of mankind from the very beginning and still demands first place in our lives today! This is not a very popular part of the gospel of Christ. Many Christians give to God, but many other "Christians" do not want to give much of anything to God—not of their dollars and not of their lives. When a crisis touches their hearts or they have an abundance of their own, some people give a little. This type of giving is not offering God anything more than the scraps we might feed our dogs (even though the vet says we shouldn't.) We don't eat scraps; we certainly don't let our children eat scraps. We mostly don't let our children do without anything they might want, let alone need. We give readily to ourselves, and we give readily to our children. So when we give God scraps, we push Him to the end of the priority list and put Him last in our lives. That's not God's way. He will never accept being pushed into the back corners of our hearts. He will be first in our lives in word and action, or He will not be in our lives at all! If we do not evidence with the giving of our time, talent, and tithe that He is really number 1, then He is not! My mom always said, "Actions speak louder than words!" God is never number 2. Are you allowing Him to be number 1 in your life?

Some people, then, say tithing is an Old Testament expectation and does not apply to us in this era. They sometimes say it is not taught in the New Testament. You may hear some of these people. You can believe these people are wrestling with God over those intimate portions of their heart and are unwilling to turn self over to the Holy Spirit! Don't despise them, but don't listen to them either! The *method* of practicing the law of God has changed but not the spiritual law of God itself. He still calls men and women into His full-time service. The church is still God's way of ministering to people in this era. He still wants to be number 1 in our lives. And tithing is still His way of funding these things and still one of His ways of focusing our lives on Him from day-to-day. What does Christ say about this? Let's look to Jesus's greatest sermon that we call the "Sermon on the Mount." In Matthew 5:17–20, NKJV, are some enlightening words on this subject.

> Do not think that I came to destroy the Law or the Prophets (Old Testament.) I did not come to destroy but to fulfill. For assuredly, I say to you, till heaven and earth pass away, one jot or tittle will by no means pass from the Law until all is fulfilled. Whoever therefore breaks one of the least of these commandments, and teaches men so, shall be called least in the kingdom of heaven; but whoever does and teaches them, he shall be called great in the kingdom of heaven. For I say unto you, that unless your righteousness exceeds the righteousness of the scribes and Pharisees, you will by no means enter the kingdom of heaven.

So Jesus came to bring completeness to what we call the Old Testament. He came to validate what was taught there to fulfill prophesy and to complete the plan of salvation. *Within the scope of that teaching, then, brought into the New Testament era, the idea of giving to God our time, our talent, and the tithe of our income is still the godly thing to do!* Some Pharisees, for instance, liked to give large sums of money when people were watching but not regular tithe. Jesus condemned them. They lived for the show and for causing people to see them and praise them. This was and is not Jesus's way. We are supposed to give not for the honor of people but out of love for and obedience to Him. He wants us to follow His tithing principle. As they came and asked questions of Him, trying to trap Him with the Romans, they asked about taxes, and He said, "Then pay Caesar what is due to Caesar, and pay God what is due to God" (Matthew 22:21, NEB). Again, some Pharisees tithed very faithfully, even on the very slightest increase of their gardens like small spices. Again then, Jesus said in Matthew 23:23–24 (ESV), "You pay tithes of mint and dill and cumin; but you have overlooked the weightier demands of the Law, justice, mercy, and good faith. It is these you should have practiced WITHOUT NEGLECTING THE OTHERS" (bold, emphasis mine). So even according to Jesus in the New Testament, tithing is still an important and necessary command today! It is still God's method for fueling the ministry of His church in the world. Our tithes and offerings do not make God rich; He already owns it all. It makes funds available for kingdom work here in this world.

Time

Time is a monstrous concern. I have often said, "Pile up all your time and pile up all your money and offer one of them to God. He will take your time, every single time!" He has and can get money everywhere. The giving of our money is an obedience issue, not a money issue. It's what we hold dear, not what God holds dear. God can take your money but can get your time only one place, only one way—from you when you choose to give it.

Since God works through the human as a method of reaching mankind, then your time and my time are important to Him and His work. "The harvest is plentiful, but the workers are few. Ask the Lord of the harvest, therefore, to send out workers into His harvest field" (Matthew 9:37–38, NIV). That job of reaching the world with the gospel is an astronomical one! The need is tremendous! The number of people who needed Christ in His day on earth was more than Jesus and His disciples were reaching. There were more needy people than the new Christian church was able to reach with its phenomenal growth over the next few years. Over the next few centuries, the number of new people being reached versus the number of new people in the world has grown farther and farther apart. A smaller and ever smaller percentage of the world is Christian every day. The harvest field grows larger, and the laborers, fewer every year. John 3:17 (KJV) says, "God sent not His Son into the world to condemn the world; but that the world (the whole world) through Him might be saved." Imagine Christ's anxiety about the number of souls slipping away into the devil's hell every day. Imagine His sorrow about His people who selfishly guard their own time rather than give it to Him and His kingdom. It's like this: we stand callously by on the edge of a swimming pool and watch as people drown well within our reach. They are screaming for help. They are thrashing around in the water. They are coughing, sputtering, and choking. They are crying and begging for help. Many "Christians" are drinking lemonade and watching the kids play soccer just a few feet away! If someone would stop for just a few moments, they could show love, reach out, and save a life. You say, "It's not really like that!" I say it is. A few moments in fervent prayer, a few minutes to show love to a child or needy person in Jesus's name, an evening here and there witnessing, could mean eternal life for many! *How can we stand idly by? How can we ever stop working for Jesus? How can we horde our time, energy, and money?* Some "Christians" never do anything! Some, selfishly, very little! Can Christ really accept that? In John 15:1–6 is the story of a vineyard. According to verse 2, God does not just accept our lack of work for the kingdom! Those who do not produce are cut off and destroyed. The Bible does not teach being saved, being filled, and sitting in the Lazy Boy rocker! We all have work to do!

Think about this. Do we owe God a tithe of our time, two hours and forty minutes a day? Chew on that one! I don't actually think the Bible demands that; however, please do not follow the example of many who call themselves "Christians" around you. Please be different for Jesus!

I warned you many people wash out here! Don't let the devil do it to you!

Money

I have already given significant coverage in this chapter to the idea of tithing, giving 10 percent to God, even giving the first 10 percent to God. I don't believe any serious follower of God will follow Him long without being confronted by Him about tithing. But there are still a couple of perspectives about tithing our money I would like to cover now. Stick with me!

In John 14:15–24 (KJV), as Jesus speaks of sending another "Helper" (v. 16), He ties that clearly to the process of obedience by mentioning four different times, "If you love Me, keep My commandments" (vv. 16, 21, 23, 24). Giving to God is one of those instructed areas, as we have already established. So as a new Christian, since you have found forgiveness of sins and allowed Jesus into your heart and are hopefully developing a real relationship with Him, let me challenge you to find those ways to obey His commandments and give to Him. Then as you find a place to pour your financial giving into, do it from a heart of love because without love, you're wasting your time and energy. Scripture tells us, "God loves a cheerful giver." Jesus is looking for us to portray Him. He *is* giving! He wants us to give from a heart of love, compassion, and obedience. John Maxwell continues this idea by saying, "People do not care how much you know until they know how much you care." You can only reach people for Jesus when you reach out in love, compassion, understanding, and acceptance. That's who Jesus is! Giving and attitude are eternally bound together! Give because you want to give; give because you love Jesus!

We have talked only about tithing so far in measuring our giving. Tithing is the rule of law. It is the minimum God requires. What can we do over and above our tithe? As David Letterman says, "One word," offerings!

Let me begin with a brief comparison. Do you, would you, only love your spouse, children, mother, to the minimum level to which you could get by? Would you only do for your children the basics of food, clothing, and shelter, and not show them any other love? What about Christmas, birthdays, Mother's Day, and hugs? What about proms, first dates, newly licensed drivers, and sleepovers? What about candies, flowers, balloons, and teddy bears? Giving just the basics to our loved ones is comparable to just tithing and never giving God anything else. Again, if you are developing that love relationship with Jesus, won't you want to show Him a level of love over and above only tithing?

There are lots of opportunities in the Christian world for giving beyond our tithe: Sunday school, your church's missionaries, the salvation army, needy people, special offerings, children's funds, etc. Also, the simple act of regularly giving "a little bit more" each time you tithe can show God your caring attitude. Give from a heart of love! I heard this comparison once: we can be like a large coffee maker where everyone gets coffee from the nozzle at the bottom. God is the eternal coffee maker who keeps pouring coffee into the top. As long as we continue to give away what He gives to us, He will continue to pour blessings into the top. Don't be afraid to give; God always gives back! As a matter of fact…

You Can't Out-Give God

In addition to giving being God's law, God also promises blessings to those who obey the law about giving. God wants us to give out of love and to be obedient, but He has this thing about never being out-given. You cannot out-give God. Because of God's great gift of His Son and the subsequent gift of eternal life, we are indebted and could never give God enough to earn such a benefit. That benefit is a gift! In addition to that, however, God is not out-given and offers blessing in return for honoring Him, in giving. Let's review just two scriptures commenting about this.

First, Proverbs 3:9–10 (NKJV) says, "Honor the Lord with your possessions, and with the first-fruits of all your increase; so your barns will be filled with plenty, and your vats will overflow with new wine." When we honor God with our possessions, which we really know belong to Him, and with the tithe of all our income, He promises blessings on our lives by way of increased possessions and income. Many times I have heard new Christians starting to tithe say, "The 90 percent goes farther than the whole check did." That is what God is saying in this Proverbs passage. Be generous toward me with what you have (offerings) and tithe on your increase (tithe) and I will cause you to always have and always increase. God's Word!

Secondly, look at Malachi (Mal-la-kai) 3:10 (NKJV). This promise seems to go even further. "'Bring all the tithes into the storehouse, that there may be food in my house, and try Me now in this,' says the Lord of Host, 'if I will not open for you the windows of heaven, and pour out for you such blessing, that there will not be room enough to receive it.'" God challenges us here! Can you believe that? God lays out a challenge to those not tithing and says, "Go ahead. Try me." God promises here to pour out blessings to an overflowing proportion when we bring all our tithes into the storehouse (the church). Other scriptures apply here as well; we must not be giving just to get (James 4:3). That would be presuming on God, perhaps lusting. Our attitude still counts. But God's Word is always kept! When we live according to His Word, those promises apply to us!

At this pastorate where I have just ended ministry, I remember my first new convert. This was a lady who had been a Christian some time before and came to me during the week, seeking to talk. She poured out her heart about the last few years and why she had not been living a Christian life. She recommitted to Christ that day, and I was able to watch her and her husband grow in the Lord over the next few years. After about a year, they came to a crisis point about tithing. They had grown to the point as Christians where they had fully submitted themselves to God in every area of their lives. They struggled only a little about giving. They had been giving, but not a full tenth, and no offerings beyond. Now they wholeheartedly recognized God's ownership of everything in their lives and began to give a full 10 percent tithe, or so they thought. After a short time, they realized they had not calculated in their rental income and began to tithe on that also. God took notice! It was fun to watch God bless these people. I'm sure I don't know all the blessings and couldn't remember them if I did. But a daughter who had left home with a less-than-stable guy came home and returned to Christ and to date, is seeking to attend Bible college. A wayward son, although still not accepting Christ, has changed His life around, graduated from a good tech school, landed a good job, and is doing well. A son-in-law from a difficult home background has made the first steps toward Christ. This couple's own relationship has matured and developed into a richer, more meaningful one. God all but handed them six acres of land with a house and two other buildings. The husband was promoted at work and given a hefty raise. And much more! All this took place within about two years of their decision to start tithing. God's Word never fails.

As a young man myself in the military, with one child and on a limited budget, I remember we were not tithing. We knew better but were so squeezed financially we just did not tithe. During a revival at the church we were attending, a husband and wife evangelistic team preached on tithing in back-to-back services. We made a decision to tithe despite the fact it was not in the budget. And we began. Almost immediately, long before we felt the budget impact, I think even within days of our decision, I was chosen for a temporary duty assignment as a hometown recruiter. I had applied but never expected to be picked for this elusive assignment. We were able to move back to our hometown, receive all our normal pay, plus $25 per day in nontaxable temporary duty pay (TDY pay.) What a blessing! Home for six months! That's right, 180 days! Four thousand five hundred dollars in nontaxable extra pay! In the mid-seventies, that was a ton of money to me! We were well able to pay off several bills and bring our budget in line to include tithing. Jesus never fails!

Beyond all this, as we move into eternal life, Jesus still does not forget our giving. That's right! We can build up eternal reward by doing and giving to Christ in this life. In Matthew 19, where Jesus is discussing eternal life with the rich young ruler, as we call Him, and then riches with His disciples, Jesus finishes that discussion with these words, "So Jesus replied, I tell you this: in the world that is to be, when the Son of Man is seated on His throne in heavenly splendor, you My followers will have thrones of your own, where you will sit as judges of the twelve tribes of Israel. And anyone who has left brothers or sisters, father, mother, or children, land or houses, for the sake of My name will be repaid many times over, and gain eternal life" (Matthew 19:28–29, NEB). You cannot out-give God ever! He wants you to give to Him and His work liberally out of a heart of love and compassion for the lost. He will always give back blessing if you are giving with the right attitude, and even sometimes when not.

I know a non-Christian farmer whose wife talked him into tithing for one year. She was a faithful Christian who wanted to give to God. That spring, his cattle had nineteen sets of twin calves! Gospel truth! You will never be able to out-give God! Enjoy the blessings of trying!

Where Do You Put

Your Time, Talent, and Tithe?

Jesus did not come into this world for only one reason, but primarily for one reason. He came to fulfill all prophecies about Himself, to start a new era of redemption for mankind by dying on the cross, for establishing a permanent method for mankind to come to know God, to establish the new church, and in Luke 19:10 (KJV), Jesus says, "For the Son of Man has come to seek and save that which was lost." Jesus came to give mankind the opportunity, our choice, to be saved from eternal damnation, which was created for the devil and His angels. Again, He works through mankind to accomplish this worldwide task. That effort deserves as much of our time, talent, and tithe as we can muster! We should give all that even without a specific call from God. I can't tell you every right or wrong place to put your efforts, and there are many rip-offs, but people and places who genuinely seek to win those who are lost are always right! Let God's Spirit be your guide! Don't give carelessly! Don't just assume because of a name, a place is biblical. There are many helps and guides. Trust your instincts and ask Jesus to guide you!

Jesus says in Matthew 28:19–20 (NIV), "Go therefore and make disciples of all the nations, baptizing them in the name of the Father, and of the Son, and of the Holy Spirit, teaching them to observe all things that I have commanded you." This is worthy of your time: winning people to Christ, baptizing them into the kingdom as a testimony of their faith, and discipling them to follow all the teachings of Christ. These things are worthy of as much energy as you can funnel into them. This is giving to God. This would include all the direct and indirect ways of which you can think. For instance, praying for missions and missionaries is a valued way to spend your time. Giving regularly to support a missionary, giving to missions in general, going on a missions work and witness team, or being a missionary are all valid ways of giving to God. However you might choose to give, specifically called into ministry or not, time, talent, or tithe, Christ's work in this world deserves our efforts! Not just from the standpoint that the work is significant, but from the standpoint of obedience to and love for Jesus Christ.

Sunday is an excellent time for giving. I know there are picnics, football games, family gatherings, and naps already scheduled on Sundays. Believe it or not, people play golf, mow grass, fish, and shop on Sunday as well. It's already a busy day in your life, I know. However, in the light of this new life you are trying to live, in light of this world wide spread-the-gospel program you have become a part of, please consider restructuring some Sundays or some Sunday time. Listen to what God says about His holy day:

> If you turn away your foot from the Sabbath, from doing your pleasure on My holy day, and call the Sabbath a delight, the holy day of the Lord honorable, and shall honor Him, not doing your own ways, nor finding your own pleasure, nor speaking your own words, then you shall delight yourself in the Lord; and I will cause you to ride on the high hills of the earth, and feed you with the heritage of Jacob your father. The mouth of the Lord has spoken. Isaiah 58:13–14 (KJV)

To rest or to worship God on His day are certainly activities that honor God. It's even hard to say that doing many of the aforementioned activities on Sunday would be wrong, especially given the right situation. That's not my point. How about considering some activities that give to God on His day? How about combining some activities you might already do with others where you give to God? Talk to someone about Jesus at that picnic. Invite someone to church with you during the football game. Take a rest and write a friend about what Jesus has recently done for you. According to this Isaiah promise, when we turn away from pleasing ourselves and do something for God on His day, we are blessed by God. We can be obedient to God, further the kingdom of God, and be blessed by God as a result of our actions all at the same time! That's powerful! That's worthy of your consideration!

So ultimately what does God want from most of us?

Self

He wants the whole of you! I said earlier in this chapter God is not second anything! He does not deserve second and does not want to be second in your life! In order for you to become all God has in store for you, the ultimate giving on your part will be necessary. Jesus gave all on the cross for you and me. Now He asks in return for us to give all to Him. In Romans 12:1–2 (NIV), we read the Apostle Paul's description of this.

> Therefore, I urge you, brothers, in view of God's mercy, to offer your bodies as living sacrifices, holy and pleasing to God—this is your spiritual act of worship. Do not conform any longer to the pattern of this world, but be transformed by the renewing of your mind. Then you will be able to test and approve what God's will is—His good, pleasing and perfect will.

This level of giving is a topic for the next book in this series, but some quick coverage here is appropriate.

Again, God wants you! He wants to take you to another level of commitment where the Holy Spirit will come to abide within you and you will be empowered to accomplish more for Him. The disciples, the first to accept the Holy Spirit in this way, experienced this in the second chapter of Acts, which we refer to as Pentecost. This is where they really became effective for God. In the last few scenes of the Gospels (Matthew, Mark, Luke, and John of the New Testament), where we see Peter, for instance, before this infilling of the Holy Spirit, he is denying Christ before a young lady who recognizes Him as a part of Jesus's group, and he becomes depressed and goes back to fishing. These are not scenes that instill us with much confidence in Peter. After this infilling and empowering of the Holy Spirit, however, we see Peter in Acts, preaching publicly to thousands in the street and thousands believing in Christ that day as a result! What a difference! In a similar manner, we can experience this today! God wants us to give up that root of self. He wants us to, as Paul puts it, "present our bodies a living sacrifice" for service to Him. This is a greater level of giving than we have discussed so far!

From the curse of Adam and Eve, man has been born with a desire to have his own way. That selfishness controls us to a great extent. God has promised to never take away our right to choose. We can choose to be selfish and have our own way, or we can choose to allow Jesus through his death on the cross to forgive us and allow His Spirit to infill us. You have probably experienced the forgiveness as you are reading this book. That is the first step! Our challenge in giving is to take the next step and to give ourselves, to turn over to God all control! This is a big and sometimes scary step. Not everyone wants to give away control, let alone all control, not even to God. Unless you take this step, however, your spiritual growth will be stymied. You will *never* be all you can be for God. God must be in control!

You don't have to take this step now, but God does not want you to avoid this knowledge! Think about it! Read about it in scripture. Pray about it. God will lead you. But God will never rush you to take a step where you are not comfortable. Take your time. This is the ultimate step of giving! Giving yourself is where God is trying to take you. Get ready for the excitement of a sold-out life to God!

10

Wolves in Sheep's Clothing

"I am astonished that you are so quickly deserting the
One who called you by the grace of Christ and are turning
to a different gospel—which is really no gospel at all.
Evidently some people are throwing you into confusion
and are trying to pervert the gospel of Christ."
—Galatians 1:6–7 (ASV)

Wolves in Sheep's Clothing

Introduction

New Christian, this chapter is an overview or summary about the Christian walk in today's world. It is very important you, as a beginner in this walk, realize the conditions of your Christian environment. What and who is around you will especially affect your beginning walk. They will also affect your eventual outcome or total growth. Just as a premature baby sometimes gets off to a slow start and is always slow or behind in some instances, so too can you spiritually unless you are aware and take steps to ensure your growth. Many premature babies do just fine! And so can you! Please read this chapter carefully and ask the Holy Spirit to guide you in this area of thought. I'm praying for your success! May God richly bless you!

There is a great laxness or coldness that permeates the overall church today! This does *not* necessary speak of your church, church people, or pastors! I cannot speak specifically about them as I do not know them. I am speaking about the overall church in the world today, particularly the American and European church. This laxness is a shallowness from which "Christians" do very little. It is a comfort zone from which "Christians" pray very little, care very little, and give very little. It is not the picture of Christ! It is not of Him! I challenge you to be like Christ and not like the majority of the church today. Look into the Garden of Gethsemane in Matthew 26:36–46, and you can see this differential between Christ and His disciples (not yet filled with the Holy Spirit). Jesus is praying about the upcoming experiences of arrest, beatings, and bearing our sins on the cross. It is excruciating! Verses 38 and 39 show His pain. Luke 22:43–44, speaking of this same incident, tells of an angel ministering to Christ, of His agony, and of His sweat as great drops of blood falling to the ground. This is the picture of One extremely concerned about you and me and our sins! Where are the disciples? They are sleeping! They cannot stay up and pray with Him for one hour! Here is the picture of Christ, driving Himself even when He, as a human, wanted to do something different; driving Himself to accept the cross and make a way of deliverance for us! That is still the picture of Christ today. He is still merciful and sacrificial and representative of us to the Father today. The disciples are still largely the picture of the church today! The church is rarely sacrificial or a praying church today. Where is the caring and concern of the church today? Who do you know who is in agony over lost souls? New Christian, do not pattern yourself after a church that's caught up in the riches and cares of this world (Matthew 13:22). There are good individual churches and Christians out there! Find some of them with which to worship and serve! Help them to make an impact in your community. Know Christ cares about your lost neighbor, a lost aunt and uncle, a lost town, and a lost world! Know Christ wants you to care and to develop your pattern for living after Him!

Try to draw some good for yourself in this area from this chapter. Don't become cynical about the church, but don't accept less than the Truth for yourself.

Good vs. Evil

Even though I briefly referred to this topic in chapter 1, let's reset the stage about good versus evil at the beginning of this chapter. Some time back before the beginning of the world as we know it, God gave to all beings then only created beings, a choice about continuing to serve Him. This seems to have been motivated by God's justice and a sense of total fairness and God's desire to have someone love and serve Him out of personal desire. These created beings were created for His purposes and had no choice before this time. The Bible doesn't make everything perfectly clear, but we can deduce some things from His actions. We know God wanted something different for several reasons. First, He gave His angels a choice. He didn't have to do this. He did this out of His own heart. He seems not to have been satisfied with His original arrangement. Second, we know He created a new level of beings and gave us a choice. That's our story and the story of the cross. Then thirdly, we are created in His likeness, and we have the same desire He has, within us. We want someone to love us out of personal desire. That power of choice, which God continues to allow, is what mankind struggles with and what cost Lucifer his position in heaven. Lucifer, the archangel, took his power of choice and, with about one-third of all the angels in heaven, tried to overthrow God's Son, Jesus (Isaiah 14:12–17, Ezekiel 28:12–19—Old Testament exposition of Lucifer/Satan—2 Peter 2:4). Lucifer was not successful, of course, but was ejected from heaven with his followers to become who we know as the devil and his angels. This world became his domain (John 21:31, Ephesians 2:2), and he will remain here until final judgment, when he will be destroyed by Christ. But for now, he remains here to fight against God, mostly by fighting us and misleading mankind.

Obviously, good and evil are ultimately represented by God and the devil respectively. They are opposites. We have discussed God's goals, John 3:16–17. God is trying to share the news of the cross and forgiveness for all with the whole world. The devil is trying to impede, slow, and even stop that effort whenever he can. God is trying through the church and Christian mankind to win and disciple every soul in the world. Second Peter 3:9 (NEB), says, "It is not that the Lord is slow in fulfilling His promise, as some suppose, but that He is very patient with you, because it is not His will that any should be lost, but for all to come to repentance." Christ is patient and tolerant and forgiving toward mankind and is trying to help us all have eternal life. His heart is broken by mankind's stubborn willfulness, which keeps people from submitting to Him. The devil is still telling current-day people the same line he told Eve. He says, "A loving God will surely not destroy you." So then, we Americans tell pollsters we believe in eternal life but not eternal death; eternal heaven but not eternal hell. Mankind hasn't learned much of anything from Eve's sin or her punishment or much from thousands of years of history as an example. Even though God has given to us the Bible as recorded documentation of His rules, many still don't care to listen or believe. Even with biblical history as a record of reward and punishment, mankind hasn't learned. The Bible itself records mankind's ah-ha moments as God did something outstanding (healed, defeated an overwhelming army, split the sea or the river, provided water in the desert, answered by fire, and so on) and also records mankind's wandering away and acts of idolatry a few years later. The devil continues to distract mankind and deny him the truth. Scripture tells us he is out for our destruction. First Peter 5:8 (NKJV) tells us, "Be sober, be vigilant, because your adversary the devil walks about like a roaring lion, seeking whom he may devour." He hates God and will destroy your soul and mine, if he can, in an effort to hurt God. The devil presents the pleasures and riches of this world to whomever will listen, on whatever level he can reach them, in an effort to keep mankind focused on this day and this life rather than on life eternal. "There is no rush to make that decision," he tells people about knowing Christ. "How about this raise or this new job or this new car," he says as he distracts people with thoughts of here and now. The devil has no boundaries, no morals, no hesitation about your destruction in this life and the next. He is like a condemned killer sentenced to life in prison; he has nothing to lose in killing again and again! He is the father of lies, the Bible tells us. If you will listen, he will ruin your marriage, your health, or damn your eternal soul. His business is to hurt God in any way he can. You will be the devil's pawn in hurting God unless you aggressively choose for God! It is a decision you will have to reaffirm over and over again. Good vs. evil. Loving parent vs. local drug dealer. God vs. the devil.

Picture yourself with a sixteen-year-old daughter; easy for me as I've done it three times over and am working on the fourth. She has grown up the apple of your eye. She is bright, in the national honor society. She is athletic, star of the high school basketball team. She is pretty, sophomore homecoming attendant. She is popular, center of attention for a great group of church kids. Life couldn't be better for her and so couldn't be better for you as a parent. She begins to take an interest in a new friend. "What's that all about?" you ask. "Just some guy who feels left out at school," she replies. You breathe easier. Her grades begin to slip. She decides not to go out for basketball her junior year. She begins to date this new guy. Your blood pressure rises. You sit down to talk. "Oh, Dad and Mom, you just don't understand." You pray. You challenge. You argue and fight with her. Things get worse, not better. Life is crashing down around her and you. Counseling doesn't work. She won't cooperate. You begin to have chest pains. You develop an ulcer. You can't sleep nights. She is out later and later. Suddenly, she is pregnant! "No, please, God. No!" you cry. Life couldn't be worse! A doctor discovers your daughter has aids! "HOW, God? HOW?"

Can you feel that frantic feeling inside you? Can you feel the pain in your heart? Can you imagine the feeling of absolute powerlessness one might feel? How about the overwhelming frustration and the desire to smash things? During the crying in the night might one want to end it all? And all this might be just a fractional glimpse of the franticness of emotion that even God must surely feel as He watches the devil wreak havoc on what was His perfect human race, from Adam and Eve all the way to now! How could a parent not have some of those frantic feelings? Even God! God is lovingly, trying to save as many of His children as He can! The devil is doing everything he can to prevent mankind from finding God and to hurt God in every way He can.

What is the future of this good-versus-evil relationship? God is ultimate power and has and will totally overcome the devil. In the end, at the last judgment, the devil will be cast into the Lake of Fire to burn forever and forever (Revelation 20:7–10). Good wins over evil. In the beginning, God overcame Lucifer fighting Christ. In the end, the Creator God of the Universe will overcome and destroy evil. In the middle, here and now, many souls are being destroyed as the evil strives to hurt the Creator God. You and I and all Christians, however, can overcome the devil with God's power and help (Revelation 12:10–11). I urge you not to become a statistic of the devil's fight against God.

Sidetracked

Let's look at some specifics about how the devil attempts to hurt God by attacking you spiritually. We have seen the good-versus-evil overview and how it turns out. How does this play out on a day-by-day basis?

The devil never quits. His hate for God is so strong he never quits trying to cause Him pain. Despite the fact he knows his eventual outcome, he goes on fighting. And he has specific goals:

1. To destroy you spiritually to the point you give up on God and follow him (the devil) into hell. That's right. God's justice system will destroy mankind, whom He loves, if

mankind chooses to live for evil rather than for good. And that is what the devil hopes for you! You specifically! He hates God! He is still trying to beat God. He wants to turn you against God. He wants you to join him in hating God. The devil will tempt you, try you, pressure you, seduce you, pay you, elevate you, make you successful, smash you, cut you, stab you in the back—anything! His goal is God. He couldn't care any less if you burn in hell forever and ever, since that will hurt God. He is going to burn. Why would he care if you do?

2. The devil's second goal is the same as his first—to hurt God. He simply takes a different approach. Here he attacks God's kingdom in this world, the church. With this approach, the devil has gotten inside God's organization and misleads many Christians through trickery. He is the Father of Lies! This is his plan! With his same Adam and Eve line about God's goodness, the devil has seduced many Christians into being lazy and selfish. They have fallen victim to him and have been tricked into believing they have no part in the worldwide plan of spreading the gospel (2 Peter 1:3–11; John 15:1–8). The devil has sold them on the idea their agenda is more important. "Surely God does not expect you to take time away from your families to do this church work," he says. "Surely God does not want you to get sick out here in the cold," he says. "Surely God has others to support this cause today," he says. "Surely you can give at another time and in another way," he says, "God is very reasonable and understands." He mixes the truth with the evil and begins to sidetrack the Christian. Then because many Christians follow other Christians instead of following God as they should, there are many wrong examples for new Christians. In this manner, the devil does not have to cause Christians or new Christians to completely fail or to sin at first; they

simply follow others down the wrong track. That's *fatal* for the sidetracked Christian or new Christian and for the overall kingdom of God. The wolf, in sheep's clothing of course, has destroyed yet another unsuspecting new Christian, and once again, God is hurt.

3. Another way the devil uses to sidetrack new Christians, especially, is through "false prophets." Jesus warned of this. In Matthew 24:4–5 (NEB), when Jesus speaks of "the end," He says, "Take care that no one misleads you. For many will come claiming my name and saying, 'I am the Messiah' and many will be misled by them." This is certainly happening in the world today. There are literally thousands of false prophets and false and misleading doctrines in the world today. This might be the Japanese poison gas bomber who actually claimed to be God or a mainline United States church that doesn't teach the whole truth. It's a minefield out there. Remembering John 14:6 (NIV), where Jesus said, "I am the way, the truth and the life. NO ONE (emphasis mine) comes to the Father except through me," one must be very careful of all the variations out there and look only to God's Word to find the truth! In 2 Timothy 2:15 (NKJV), Paul challenges us to, "Be diligent to present yourself approved unto God, a worker who does not need to be ashamed, rightly dividing the word of truth." Therein is what the new Christian must seek; truth in the Word of God. Be able to protect yourself from the false prophet and the false teaching or teaching omission by knowing the Word. Don't lean so strongly on the word of others, where you can be misled. Paul again, because there were so many false teachings in his day, challenging the new Christians, says in Phil-lip-pe-ends 2:12 (NKJV), "Therefore, my beloved, as you have always obeyed, not as in my presence only, but now much more in my absence, work out your own salvation with

fear and trembling; for it is God who works in you both to will and to do for His good pleasure." Paul is challenging the new Christians of his day, while he is not with them, to get somewhat established on their own. He tells them to trust God, who is working within them, and not to trust so much on him. Just as with the new Christian of Paul's day, this time is fraught with many pitfalls for you, and you need to establish yourself in the Word. Depend on God and don't give the devil the opportunity to mislead you by being unprepared. That's your calling! That's your choice. Make a habit of a regular pattern of Bible *study*!

Paul again, in challenging the new Christians at Thessalonica, writes to them and says in 1 Thessalonians (Thess-a-lone-knee-ands) 5:19–22 (NKJV), "Do not quench the Spirit. Do not despise prophecies. Test all things; hold fast to what is good. Abstain from every form of evil." Let me paraphrase these four verses. Obey the Spirit of God (v. 19). Every time He says stop, stop! When He says read on, keep reading. When He says go to the altar and pray, go! Whatever the Spirit of God prompts you to do, do! Don't make fun of or look down your nose at or ignore the preaching of God's Word when God's Spirit is in it (v. 20). Pay attention and learn. Test everything you hear preached and taught with the Bible (v. 21)! Preaching and teaching must be backed up by the Bible without taking the scripture out of the context of the whole, if you are to embrace it. Discard what you hear that is not backed by the Bible; hold on to what good you hear if it is from God's Word, the Bible. Don't look at evil (v. 21). Don't participate in evil. Don't talk with evil. Don't associate with evil. Don't be part of evil in any way!

I know there are likely questions this paraphrase brings up. "How do I recognize God's Spirit? What does it mean to 'take out of context'? How do I decide what is evil?" Slow down, new Christian, it all takes time. But first, realize Paul is challenging new Christians to test what they hear against what they know is truth. It is your eternal soul. It is your responsibility to act to protect it. God will certainly do His part, but don't expect Him to do it all. Just like young children have to learn to tie their own shoes, with teaching from adults, you must learn to "rightly divide the word of truth" for yourself after basic training. There is no other way to survive. The devil will find a way to deceive you with false prophets and false teachings otherwise.

God found you and drew you to Himself, somehow. Trust Him! Then trust your basic spiritual instincts, testing what you are unsure of against the Bible. And find a mentor or discipler. But depend upon them with caution, not to the point of mistrusting them, but with caution enough to value and protect your own soul! The wolf is out there in sheep's clothing, and he is after you!

Christlikeness

The goal of this chapter was to help protect you against those hidden things the devil will use against you. I hope I have discussed some of those things in a way to benefit you. The greatest protection you can possibly have, however, is due some distinct discussion. With all your heart, strive to be as much like Christ as you can! You cannot go wrong if you are truly seeking Jesus! Let me say that again: you *cannot* go wrong if you are truly seeking Jesus in your heart! Study *His* life. Learn *His* character. Know *His* ways. Seek *His* face. Find *His* motives. Covet *His* manner. Worm into *His* heart. Imprint upon your mind *His* Word. Drink in *His* Spirit. Hunger and thirst after *His* righteousness. Ask for *His* wisdom. Lust for *His* love. Cry for *His* grace. Grasp for *His* goodness. Plunge into *His* favor. Glean *His* knowledge. Develop the fruit of *His* Spirit. Allow *His* Spirit to transform your thinking. Give with *His* generosity. Succumb to *His* stillness. Respond to *His* guidance. Desire *His* likeness. You get the idea! Become a person oozing with the Spirit of God. If you are busy truly becoming like Jesus, you will be less likely to be caught up in a trap of the devil's making.

Remember Jesus is a being of the heart—meaning what you see is what you get. Jesus's actions when here on earth were not different than how He feels in His heart today! When He walked here on earth, He did not heal for the media; He did not raise the dead without purpose. I'm trying to say, you need to be in your heart what you represent in public. God is not looking for you to mimic His actions; He is interested in you becoming like Him from within. So when I say become a reflection of Christ, I mean from within. Allow Him to transform your body, soul, and spirit, and you will become like Him.

Again, don't be sidetracked! It's probably the devil's most effective weapon. Many times in the writing and rewriting of this first book, I have had to remind myself or be reminded to stay on topic. In my desire to share all I can with new Christians, I have had the tendency to elaborate or get sidetracked onto a topic different than where I was. I have had the tendency to get sidetracked and not be writing at all. It's an easy thing to do spiritually also. Someone offends you, and the bad feelings begin (Matthew 13:21). It's that easy to wander away from where God wants you. Be careful! Be focused! Be Christlike!

> Likewise you younger people, submit yourselves to your elders. Yes, all of you be submissive to one another, and be clothed with humility, for 'God resist the proud, But gives grace to the humble.' Therefore humble yourselves under the mighty hand of God, that He may exalt you in due time, casting all your care upon Him, for He cares for you. Be sober, be vigilant; because your adversary the devil walks about like a roaring lion, seeking whom he may devour. Resist him, steadfast in the faith, knowing that the same sufferings are experienced by your brotherhood in the world. But may the God of all grace, who called us to His eternal glory by Christ Jesus, after you have suffered

awhile, perfect, establish, strengthen, and settle you. To Him be the glory and dominion forever and ever. Amen. 1 (Peter 5:8–11, NKJV)

Conclusion

Well, new Christian, you have finished this first book! However, you are just beginning the walk with God! There is so much more to come. It is going to be an exciting time! Let me have a few moments to cover some closing thoughts.

Remember, God is working in your behalf. He wants you to grow and become a strong Christian. He will help you defeat the devil every single time you allow Him. He is a majority! Paul says in Romans 8:31 (KJV), "If God be for us, who can be against us?" This does not mean the devil will not get in his licks; he will. He does not have to win! Ever!

God wants you to move forward. He wants you to grow and produce (John 15). If He leads you to do such and such and you don't, don't expect Him to lead you on to something else. He won't. He is looking for obedience. That is the key. He won't lead on until you accomplish the task first given. He won't continue to bless if you are not obeying.

But you won't have to hurry the process. A steady growth process is what will serve you best. Don't feel you need to be at the place where older, more-experienced Christians are, today. Give yourself time to get there. The devil will try to hurry you to get you to make a mistake. You don't need to slowly drag your feet, and neither do you need to race ahead at breakneck speed. You're looking for steady progress.

I'm sure, at this stage, you have many questions. You should have questions. Go back through this book, rereading areas of concern. Go to your pastor and ask questions. Look for answers in your Bible reading and Bible study. Make a study of the topic until you have your answers. This is "work out your own salvation with fear and trembling" (Philippians 2:12, NKJV).

Don't give up without an answer. Don't be satisfied with someone else's answer without supporting scripture. Know this for yourself! You need the firm foundation! Pray about this! Meditate and listen for God's voice as you read scripture. This is your chance to grow and develop. Just as we have all heard about how the not-yet-hatched chick gains necessary strength as they poke themselves out of the egg, so too can you gain necessary strength in this question and find the answer process. Don't quit!

At this particular stage of your development, growth is the key. For you to study, read your Bible, pray, attend church and Sunday school classes, attend a Bible Study or new-Christian classes, or do anything that will supplement your spiritual growth; these may be critical to your spiritual survival. Don't undervalue this necessary process. Don't let the devil cause you to give up! Mistakes will happen! You will not be perfect! You will hurt someone with an unkind word or unkind act or at least they will perceive unkindness. You will miss church. You will miss a class or a prayer time or not read your Bible as you should. You will slip back to an old habit of swearing or whatever. Be sincere and God will forgive you! The only thing that can defeat you is you quitting. As long as you make a legitimate effort, God will be there to help, forgive, and support. Don't ever quit! Depend upon God!

I once heard a story about an old forty-niner gold miner who had gone to California on news of the first strike. He had staked a claim and dug and dug. He consistently made a little money but never hit the big mother lode. He finally grew tired of others striking it rich and sold his claim to a newcomer. As he was still packing it all up the next day, the newcomer struck the mother lode in his old claim. You can never know what's just beyond the next bend in the spiritual road. Some days will look bleak and dismal. The devil will come to do battle. But you do know what is at the end of this spiritual road! Eternal life with Jesus Christ is the reward awaiting us! Don't ever quit!

Know too, new Christian, you have just begun to scratch the spiritual surface. God has great things in store for you. Whatever your road to heaven, if you will continually dedicate yourself to God and His work, spiritual depth, excitement, and satisfaction will come your way. I'm praying for you! Press on!

Study Guides

The following study outlines are meant for help in personal study, teaching, class work, etc…There is one basic outline for each chapter. They are not in-depth study, only simple outlines to aid in memory and connection with the material. New Christian, I hope these help!

1
Your Commitment

Outline:
  Spiritual History
  Justification-Forgiveness
  Sincerity
  Family of God
  Importance of the Step You Have Taken
  Public Witness of Becoming a Christian
  Baptism
  Begin to Live Christ-like
  Depend Upon Christ

Spiritual History

Read for background:
  Genesis chapters 1–3
  2 Peter 2:4
  Romans 7:14–25; Romans 5:12–14

1. What one limitation did God give to Adam and Eve in the Garden of Eden?

   _____

2. Who was the devil before he became the enemy of God?

   _____

3. List eight results of the curse on Adam and Eve and subsequently on all mankind.

   _____

   _____

_____
_____
_____
_____
_____
_____

4. Now what is the natural inclination of mankind and why?
_____
_____

Justification-Forgiveness

Read for background:
 Noah: Genesis 6–8
 Abram: Genesis 12–23
 Crucifixion: John 18–19
 Salvation: Romans 3:23, 6:23, and Revelations 3:20

5. How do you know Jesus died for you and your sins?
_____
_____
_____

6. Have you asked Jesus to forgive you of your sins and accepted Him into your heart?
 ____ yes   ____ no

7. How do you know Jesus is in your heart?
_____
_____

8. What is God's penalty for disobedience to Him?

9. What does justification mean in literal terms?

   Read: Isaiah 1:18

10. Do you have to continue to sin? ____ yes ____ no (1 John 3:4–10)

Sincerity

1. How do we know God cannot be fooled and really always knows the truth? (Hebrews 4:13; 1 John 3:20)

2. Where does God look to know the truth about us? (1 Samuel 16:7) _____

3. How many times would you allow someone to slap you?

Family of God

1. As a member and heir of God, what do you now stand to inherit? _____

2. Who are your brothers and sisters in Christ?

Importance of the Steps You Have Taken

Read: Hebrews 11

All those people are in heaven and have been for the past several thousand years. They made their decisions about God with eternity in mind.

1. What is eternity?
   _____

2. How long does it last?
   _____

3. Have you made this decision about Christ with eternity in mind? ____ yes ____ no

4. Can you list any other decision you have or will ever make that is as important as this one? ____ yes ____ no

5. List five things you are prepared to do to keep Christ in your life.
   _____
   _____

Public Witness of Becoming a Christian

Read: Matthew 10:32–33; John 15:1–8

1. Does God require you to stand on a street corner and preach in order to be a Christian? ____ yes ____ no

2. Will God let you be a secret Christian and never have any impact on anyone?
   ____ yes ____ no

Somewhere in the middle of these two extremes, where you and God are comfortable, He will expect you to impact those around you.

3. Where would you be today if someone had not told you about the love of Jesus?

4. What does it mean to "bear fruit?"

Baptism

1. Baptism is an _____ sign of an _____ work.

2. Does the Bible indicate there should only be one method of baptism?

3. Why should one invite unsaved friends and family to their baptism?

Read: Matthew 3:13–17; Luke 3:21–22

Begin to Live Christ-like

1. Does God have a strict timetable of spiritual growth outlined for everyone, or is growth based on our desire, motivation, and personalized relationship with Christ?

2. Does God wish us to grow?

3. Name ten character traits of Jesus that we might strive to have in our lives?

_____
_____

Read: James 4:8

4. What objects in our homes we all look at every day describe how we should reflect Christ?

_____
_____

People should be able to look at us and see Jesus (2 Corinthians 2:14–15). This is a goal we will always want to strive toward. However, just like becoming an eagle scout, it will take time to get there.

Depend Upon Christ

1. What is the grand paradox of the Bible?

_____
_____

2. Why would Christ want us to depend upon Him?
   Read: Matthew 28:18; Luke 1:36; Hebrews 4:13; Peter 5:81; John 8:44

_____
_____

3. Name five areas of your life where you can begin to depend upon Christ.

_____
_____

2
Prayer

Outline:
  Introduction
  Who and What
  Conversation
  When
  How
  Why
  Faith/Belief/Trust
  Scriptural Power: Prayer Promises
  What is the single most important aspect of the Christian walk? _____

Prayer: Who and What

1. Can God converse with us? _____ yes _____ no
   Read: 1 Samuel 14; Judges 6–7:15; Acts 10:9–23

2. What does the Bible say about who we should talk with as a higher power?
   Exodus 20:5–6; Matthew 4:10
   _____

3. How would you describe prayer at this point?
   _____
   _____
   _____

Conversation

1. Name five things God might like to hear from you.
   _____
   _____
   _____
   _____
   _____

   Read: Psalm 51; Psalm 47; Matthew 6:9–13

2. In your words, why might it be important to listen to God?
   _____
   _____

Prayer: When

1. How quickly each day do we greet friends or family around us and how does that reflect on how soon each day we might greet our friend Jesus?
   _____
   _____

2. When does Paul challenge us to pray in 1 Thessalonians 5?
   _____

3. Why would one schedule a private time alone with God?
   _____

   Read Jesus's example: Matthew 6:6; James 4:8

4. Finish this quote: "You will not find depth of relationship with God until you _____
   _____."

5. Why would preparation times be important times to spend with God in prayer?

   _____

   _____

Prayer: Where

1. Did Jesus have an "alone" relationship with His father?
   ___ yes ___ no

2. Does Scripture encourage us to get alone with our Father in prayer?
   ___ yes ___ no

3. What is built between us and God when we get alone with Him?

   _____

4. Does this intimate relationship simply occur, or is it purposely built by us with God?

   _____

5. What are three ingredients used in the building of this intimate relationship?
   1. _____ 2. _____
   3. _____

6. From what physical positions of prayer will God hear us?

   _____

   _____

7. List five reasons why journaling may be a good idea in conjunction with your prayer time.

_____
_____
_____
_____
_____

Prayer: How

1. What is the key word when approaching God in prayer?
   _____

2. God commands that we not use His name "_____
   _____."
   Which means _____
   _____.

3. Why was the priest struck down for touching the ark?
   _____
   What does that say about God? _____
   _____.

4. When does something we are praying about come to mean a great deal to God?
   _____

5. After sincerity, what is the next step in showing God we are serious? _____

6. We become the most effective person of prayer about topics that are what?
   _____

7. In your own words, give a brief description of faith.
   _____

8. Why does one have to look at all the scriptures about any particular topic in order to properly understand what God is saying about that topic?
   _____
   _____

9. Are there prayer "shortcuts?" ____ yes ____ no

10. Discuss how prayer formulas help us to be direct with God and to cover all the bases.
    _____
    _____
    _____

Sincerity

1. What three stories in Scripture tell us that God is serious and wants us to treat Him as such?
   a. _____
   b. _____
   c. _____

2. Who is the most important person in your family when it comes to being sincere in prayer about family?
   _____

Faith/Belief/Trust

1. Faith the size of what seed Jesus said would move mountains?
   _____

2. Look up a mustard seed online and find the actual size.

Scriptural Power: Prayer Promises

1. What short cuts are there to effectiveness with God?
   _____

2. Is it important to view all of scripture about any certain topic?
   _____

Prayer: Why

1. Name three reasons why I think prayer is important to new Christians.
   _____
   _____
   _____

2. What was Mr. Harting's prayer?
   _____

Note

1. Finish this quote: "Pray specific prayers; _____
   _____."

2. What does that mean in your everyday life?
   _____
   _____

3
Faith

Outline:
   Definitions
   History
   Developing Our Faith

Definitions

1. In your own words, please define faith.

   _____
   _____
   _____

2. What are the three dictionary definitions of faith listed in this chapter?

   _____
   _____
   _____

3. In believing in and trusting in Him, God is asking you to take a _____ of faith?

4. Read Hebrews 11 for background on other's faith.

5. Does God count on us to "expect" His answers?
   ____ yes ____ no

   How would you be demonstrating faith in God if you prayed and did not expect an answer? _____
   _____

6. According to Matthew 17:20, how much faith do we need to get God to answer?
   _____

7. Does faith come as automatic to everyone, or do we sometimes have to build our faith?
   _____

8. What is referred to, in this chapter, as the "grand paradox" of the Bible?
   _____

9. In Matthew 6:19–34, is God asking us to trust Him for the big crisis of life or for the everyday needs of life?
   _____

10. What does that level of interest say to us about God's desire for personal involvement with us?
    _____

4
Sharing Your God

Outline:
   Introduction
   God's Command
   What Others Do (Or Not Do)
   How to Share
   Motivation to Share

Introduction

1. Without training, help, and grace from God, is sharing something He expects of every new Christian?
   ____ yes ____ no

2. Is sharing God supposed to be a "scary thing?"
   ____ yes ____ no

3. God only expects sharing from us when what three preliminary things are in place?

   _____

   _____

   _____

God's Command

1. Read Matthew 28:19–20.
   Write this command in your own words.

   _____

   _____

   _____

2. With this command from Matthew to spread God's Word and God's promises from John 15, how is God like a good father?

   _____

3. Read John 3:16–17.
   Referencing these scriptures, is it God's will for your loved ones to become Christians? ____ yes ____ no

4. Chapters 1 and 2 of Acts describe the coming of the Holy Spirit into the world as one who empowers us to do the will of God. Read Matthew 26:69–74 and Acts 1–2 and describe how Peter changed and what he did as a result of that change.

   _____

   _____

5. According to Ephesians 2:19–22, what is God's plan?

   _____

What Others Do (Or Not Do)

1. Why is it important to look at Christ for an example instead of looking at other Christians?

   _____

   _____

2. Read Matthew 25:31–46.
   Will there be people who believe they are going to heaven but in judgment, find they have missed the mark?
   ____ yes ____ no

3. Read Acts 3:1–11.
   What actions of those in the world around you cause you to believe people are still looking to receive something from Christians today? _____

How to Share

1. What are the three basic types of sharing the "good news" with others?
   _____

2. When you share "your story" with someone, who is helping you?
   a. _____ b. _____ c. _____

3. When you share "your story" with someone, is their response guaranteed? Will they immediately become a Christian?
   ____ yes ____ no

4. Do you have the responsibility to cause someone to come to Christ or to affect them with your life and testimony toward Christ? _____

5. As a new Christian, until you are more spiritually mature, what two sharing methods will you most likely use?
   a. _____ b. _____

Motivation to Share

1. Beyond the command to share and Christ's example to share, what are the motivations to share as presented in this section?
   _____
   _____

2. Try to list as many people as possible who are responsible in part for your coming to Christ.
   _____
   _____

The Discipleship Series: Book One

5
Bible Study/Devotions

Outline:
   Introduction
   Devotions
   Bible Study
   Why
   How
   When
   Where

Introduction

1. Devotions are times of private _____.

2. What makes devotions so important?
   _____
   _____

3. Why is the Parable of the Soils or Sower (Matthew 13:1–9, 18–23) important to this topic?
   _____
   _____

Devotions

1. What four components of devotions are discussed in this section?
   _____
   _____

2. How much time per day is a good starting point for devotions?

Bible Study

1. Why is it necessary for us to study God's Word?

2. How is a spiritual infant similar to a human infant?

3. Who does John 14:26 indicate will teach us as we study God's Word?

4. What is the first practical step in studying God's Word?

5. What two attitudes make Bible study most effective?

6. How often should one try to study?

7. How might time spent studying the Bible be a part of what is spoken of in Revelation 3:15–16?

8. What word best describes where you might most effectively have Bible study?

6
Christian Associations

Outline:
    Introduction
    Your Are Your Environment
    Reward / Defeat
    Nature
    Association Controls

Introduction

Please reread the introduction.

1. What is the purpose of addressing this area of the new Christian's life?

2. Describe the progression of direction in Psalms 1:1:

3. According to Psalms 1:2, what would God rather us do?

4. If we allow ourselves to be re-involved in places, relationships, and activities displeasing to God, will He force us to stop?

5. Why might God want us to keep our old relationships on some level?

Nature

1. What is the positive and negative side of the natural process of associations when you are a new Christian?
   Positive: _____
   _____
   _____

   Negative: _____
   _____
   _____

2. In Mark 8:36–37, Jesus places what value on the soul of a man? _____

3. In your view, whose soul is the most important of all people in the world? _____

4. Who has the ultimate responsibility for the state of your soul?
   _____

5. Finish this quote: "You will not win your friends to Christ by _____."

6. List the five guidelines given in this chapter for associations with "old friends" now that you are a new Christian.
   a. _____
   b. _____
   c. _____
   d. _____
   e. _____

7. Leading someone to Christ is a cooperative effort at least between what four individuals?
   a. _____ c. _____
   b. _____ d. _____

Reward/Defeat

1. Why is this time as a new Christian a good time to win your non-Christian friends and family?
   _____
   _____

2. What are some things you can do for your non-Christian friends and family?
   _____
   _____

3. What is the one thing you should never do for your non-Christian friends and family?
   _____
   _____

Association Controls

1. What are the eight "controls" listed at the end of this chapter?
   a. _____
   b. _____
   c. _____
   d. _____
   e. _____
   f. _____
   g. _____
   h. _____

7
Be Conscious of God's Leadership

Outline:
    Introduction
    God's Plan for Your Life
    The Dependency Paradox
    How This Works Against Us
    Finding God's Will
    Formula for Knowing God's Will
    God Will Not Forsake You
    Listen and Obey

1. Finish this quote: "God will never lead you in a way _____ ."

2. What two kinds of God's will did you read of in the introduction?
    a. _____ b. _____

God's Plan for Your Life

1. How do we come to be trusted by God to fulfill specific plans for our lives?

2. We are challenged to live as closely to the general plan and to listen for what?

3. What plan does 2 Timothy 2:15 give to each of us to accomplish?

4. What is the final authority in this world?
   _____

5. Are there any exceptions to this rule? _____ yes _____ no

6. Do we have to face the literal devil himself very often in temptations or spiritual battles? _____ yes _____ no

7. In the example given in this chapter, why would you recognize your mother's voice?
   _____

8. Long-term specific leadership in one's life is many times referred to as "_____."

The Dependency Paradox

1. What is the dependency paradox?
   _____
   _____

How This Works Against Us

1. Explain what 2 Corinthians 12:9 says about this.
   _____
   _____

2. Finish the quote: "You must realize that on your best _____
   _____."

3. How does the dependency paradox work against us?
   _____

Finding God's Will

1. What do scriptures like Matthew 6:8–9 and 11:28 and James 1:5 prove about this topic?
   _____
   _____

2. What principle about this topic does James 4:3 teach?
   _____
   _____

3. According to John 9:31, to whom does God listen?
   _____
   _____

Formula for Knowing God's Will

1. What principle is taught in Matthew 6:8 and 7:7 about knowing God's will?
   _____
   _____

2. What three principles should we acknowledge as we begin to seek God's will?
   a. _____
   b. _____
   c. _____

3. Why is "just praying about it" and "depending on my feelings" probably not the best way?
   _____
   _____

4. In light of 1 Corinthians 14:23, does God generally rush people to make decisions? _____ yes _____ no

5. What are the four major ways of knowing God's will?
   a. _____
   b. _____
   c. _____
   d. _____

6. In Judges 7:9–14, what does God do for Gideon to reassure him of God's leadership, even when Gideon does not ask?
   _____
   _____

God Will Not Forsake You

1. According to 2 Samuel 11 and again in 12:25 and in John 8:1–11, what principle does God's Word teach, even when one has sinned?
   _____
   _____

2. How is the slap story from an earlier chapter applicable here?
   _____
   _____

Listen and Obey

1. What is the challenge of this last section of this chapter?
   _____
   _____

8
Your Pastor/Discipler

Outline:
    Roles of the Pastor / Discipler
    Nursery Attendant
    Counselor
    Teacher
    Christ, the Discipler
    Your Roles
    Watch Christ

Roles of the Pastor/Discipler

1. In 1 Corinthians 9:19–23, what principle is taught concerning your pastor/discipler?

2. Who is ultimately responsible for your salvation and discipleship?

3. Where do new Christians attend church?

4. What relationship is critical to you at this stage of your spiritual life?

Nursery Attendant

1. In 1 Peter 5:8, scripture teaches the devil has what in mind for you as a new Christian?
   _____

2. Describe the relationship you should have with your pastor/discipler from this section?
   _____
   _____

3. Who should you look to in order to get questions answered about spiritual food, spiritual recreation, Christians associations, etc.?
   _____

4. Are there those "out there," who you should be afraid will mislead you spiritually? _____ yes _____ no

Counselor

1. What types of questions should you be able to ask your discipler?
   _____

2. As in any field of training, is there any stupid question you could formulate?
   _____

Teacher

1. Where is the most ideal teaching/learning spot for you?
   _____
   _____

2. In this light, when should you be prepared to learn from your discipler?

   _____
   _____

3. Can it be beneficial to you to watch your discipler's life for how they live life? _____ yes _____ no

4. Is this a possibly dangerous relationship for you, and if so, why? _____ yes _____ no

   _____

Christ, the Discipler

1. What method did Christ use when training the disciples?

   _____
   _____

2. List some other learning times you could spend with your discipler.

   _____
   _____

3. Are there any limitations placed upon spending time with your discipler?

   _____
   _____

Your Roles

1. At this stage of your Christian walk, what is your primary role?

   _____
   _____

2. Describe in this role as a student, how you can be like a sponge?
   _____
   _____

3. Can your discipler ever be wrong? _____ yes _____ no

4. Should this role of student and sponge be without limitations, without checks and balances? _____ yes _____ no

Watch Christ

1. Our real goal is to be like _____.

2. To become Christlike will take "_____ _____ and _____ on your part."

3. Describe how it is that Christ expects us to be a peculiar people.
   _____
   _____

9
Giving to God

Outline:
  Author's Challenge
  Again, God's Plan for the World: Your Part
  Time
  Money
  You Can't Out-Give God
  Where Do You Put Your Time, Talent, and Tithe?
  Self

Author's Challenge

1. Follow the challenge. Stop at the beginning of this chapter and spend some time in prayer asking God to strengthen you and to defeat the devil in your life.

2. What is the inference of the value of a soul according to Matthew 16:24–26?

   _____

   _____

Again, God's Plan for the World: Your Part

1. According to John 3:16–17, what is God's plan for the whole world?

   _____

2. In 2 Corinthians 5:14–15, explain what you think Paul means when he says, "Live no longer for themselves."

   _____

3. What is the first principle of giving?
   _____

4. If then God owns everything, what position of responsibility does that put us in?
   a. none   b. stewardship

5. What is the second principle of giving?
   _____

6. Where are we primarily taught to put that tenth part? Into the _____.

7. Who is the first tither in scripture?
   _____

Actually, no. This was a trick question. Early in Genesis 4, Cain and his brother, Able, bring offerings to God, which could be considered a tithe. Scripture even says Able brought the "firstlings" of his flocks.

8. According to Numbers 18:20, the tribe of Levi received no land for inheritance as did all other tribes. Why?
   _____
   _____

9. How does God's pattern of tithing work to supply church and ministers their "inheritance" today?
   _____
   _____

10. What is the third principle of giving?
    _____

11. What does this principle mean when we are paying our bills each pay period?
   _____

12. Does God ever accept second or last place in our lives? _____ yes _____ no

13. If you don't already know it, memorize what Mom always says, "Actions speak louder than words."

14. Find a scripture other than Matthew 5:17–20, referred to in this chapter, that shows that Christ came to fulfill the Old Testament law, not to destroy it.
   _____

15. Take a moment to figure your tithe (10%). There is no need to share this with anyone, but now you will know what God expects of you.

Time

1. How is the only way for God to get your time?
   _____

2. Do a little outside study here. Try to find out the population of the world in Jesus's day. What is the population of the world now? Jesus began with twelve disciples, so try to find out the number of themselves Christians today and compare percentages. Are we gaining or losing?

3. Make a list of ten (10) non-Christian people for who you can begin to pray.
   1. _____
   2. _____
   3. _____
   4. _____

5. _____
6. _____
7. _____
8. _____
9. _____
10. _____

Money

1. In John 14:15–24, Jesus speaks of obeying Him if we love Him. List four commandments of Christ, other than the Ten Commandments, to which this passage could apply.
   a. _____
   b. _____
   c. _____
   d. _____

2. Name two situations from your church or community to which John Maxwell's quote would apply.
   a. _____
   b. _____

3. Explain the difference between tithe and offering:
   _____

Can't Out-Give God

1. Name another scripture besides what is discussed in the book that promises reward for giving to God.
   _____

2. Do you have or know of a "can't out-give God" story? Relate it here. _____
   _____
   _____

Where Do You Put Your Time, Talent, and Tithe?

1. What was Jesus's primary reason for coming into this world?
   _____
   _____

2. Name five (5) of your "pleasures" you are enjoying on His holy day:
   a. _____
   b. _____
   c. _____
   d. _____
   e. _____

3. Name five things you might do for God on His holy day:
   a. _____
   b. _____
   c. _____
   d. _____
   e. _____

Self

1. What does Romans 12:1 ask us to do?
   _____

2. By comparing your love relationship with God to a human relationship you have or have had, explain why God wants all of you rather than share you with "self."
   _____
   _____

3. I encourage you to continue to pray and be open-minded about this issue of infilling or holiness. Listen for God's voice.

10
Wolves in Sheep's Clothing

Outline:
   Introduction
   Good Vs. Evil
   Sidetracked
   Christlikeness

Introduction

1. What is the overall general condition of today's church?

2. What do those terms *coldness* or *laxness* mean?

3. From a "caring about us" point of view, describe what was motivating Jesus to go through what He did leading up to and including the cross.

Good Vs. Evil

1. What act on God's part caused the beginning of the good-versus-evil scenario?

2. What three reasons show us God wanted something different than just beings that had to worship Him?
   a. _____
   b. _____
   c. _____

3. From John 3:17, what is God's plan for the world?
   _____
   _____

4. From Matthew 29:19–20, what is God's plan, concerning the world, for those of us in the church today?
   _____
   _____

5. Explain in your own words 1 Peter 5:8.
   _____
   _____

6. Explain in your own words how the devil fights to hurt God.
   _____
   _____